GLADWYNE FREE LIBRARY
Gladwyne, PA 19035

Best Easy Day Hikes
Acadia National Park

D0683992

Best Easy Day Hikes Series

Best Easy Day Hikes
Acadia
National Park

Fourth Edition

Dolores Kong and Dan Ring

FALCONGUIDES

GUILFORD, CONNECTICUT

FALCONGUIDES®

An imprint of The Rowman & Littlefield Publishing Group, Inc.
4501 Forbes Blvd., Ste. 200
Lanham, MD 20706
www.rowman.com

Falcon and FalconGuides are registered trademarks and Make
Adventure Your Story is a trademark of The Rowman & Littlefield
Publishing Group, Inc.

Distributed by NATIONAL BOOK NETWORK

Copyright © 2019 The Rowman & Littlefield Publishing Group, Inc.

A previous edition of this book was published by Falcon Publishing, Inc.
in 2001, 2011, and 2015.

Maps by Melissa Baker

All rights reserved. No part of this book may be reproduced in any
form or by any electronic or mechanical means, including information
storage and retrieval systems, without written permission from the
publisher, except by a reviewer who may quote passages in a review.

British Library Cataloguing in Publication Information available

Library of Congress Cataloging-in-Publication Data available

ISBN 978-1-4930-4061-2 (paperback)
ISBN 978-1-4930-4062-9 (e-book)

∞™ The paper used in this publication meets the minimum
requirements of American National Standard for Information
Sciences—Permanence of Paper for Printed Library Materials, ANSI/
NISO Z39.48-1992.

Printed in the United States of America

The authors and The Rowman & Littlefield Publishing Group, Inc. assume
no liability for accidents happening to, or injuries sustained by, readers who
engage in the activities described in this book.

Contents

The Hikes

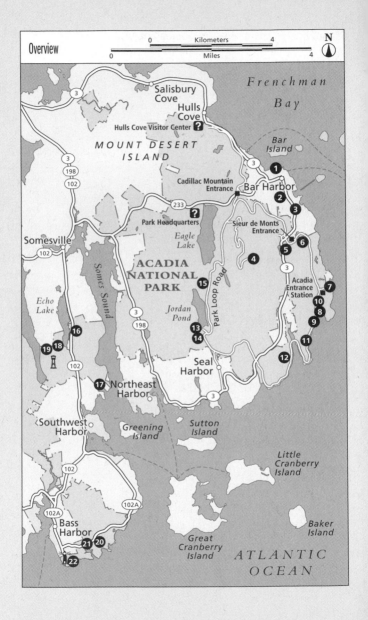

Acknowledgments

For sharing their knowledge and passion for Acadia National Park, and for being so generous with their time, we'd like to thank Wanda Moran, Charlie Jacobi, Gary Stellpflug, Christian Barter, Jeff Chapin, Bruce Connery, Lynne Dominy, Vincent Sproul, John Kelly, Christie Anastasia, David Manski, Kathy Grant, Stuart West, Karen Anderson, Anne Warner, Maureen Fournier, and the rest of the Acadia National Park staff, past and present; Margaret Coffin Brown of the National Park Service; Ann Marie Cummings of Eastern National; Jill Weber; Marla S. O'Byrne; Gerry Fournier; Michael Good; Susan Hayward; Tim Henderson; Jim Linnane; Jack Russell; and the Friends of Acadia.

And we'd like to thank family and friends who've already hiked the trails of Acadia with us, or one day will: April, Thomas, Sharon, Michelle, Judy, Stacey, Jen, Phil, Sebastian, Miranda, Laura, Mike, Jenna, and Winston, and too many others to name.

Introduction

Maine's Acadia National Park is a place like no other.

You can stroll along Ocean Path and be awestruck by the contrast of pink-granite cliffs, blue skies, and white surf. From atop Cadillac, the highest mountain on the US Atlantic Seaboard, you can see fog rolling in over Frenchman Bay below, even as the sun shines brightly above. And over on the shores of Jordan Pond, you can take part in one of the most civilized of afternoon rituals, tea and popovers, with the distinct mountains known as the Bubbles as nature's backdrop.

No wonder artists, millionaires, generations of families, and even presidents—notably Barack Obama in 2010—have been attracted to all that's preserved in Acadia.

In fact, the place means so much to area residents and visitors that Acadia in 1919 became the first national park created east of the Mississippi, after starting as a national monument in 1916. It is also the first national park to consist primarily of privately donated lands, and the first to have trail maintenance funded by an endowment, Acadia Trails Forever, coming from $4 million in park user fees and federal appropriations and $9 million in private donations from Friends of Acadia, a private nonprofit organization based in Bar Harbor.

Over the years the scenery here has inspired such passion that nineteenth-century painters Thomas Cole and Frederic Church, of the Hudson River School, came here to capture the landscape; one of the wealthiest men in America, John D. Rockefeller Jr., donated millions and left miles of picturesque carriage roads and uniquely designed stone bridges; and prime mover George B. Dorr dedicated his life and exhausted his family fortune to create the park.

The scenery at Acadia even drew President Barack Obama and his family in July 2010 to the views from the top of Cadillac and along the Ship Harbor and Bass Harbor Head Light Trails.

The year 2019 marks the hundredth anniversary of Acadia's establishment as a national park, although the big centennial took place in 2016, celebrating its founding as the Sieur de Monts National Monument in 1916. The motto on the Acadia Centennial logo unveiled in 2014 was "Celebrate Our Past, Inspire Our Future."

Today more than 3 million visitors a year make Acadia one of the top-ten most visited national parks, even though it's the thirteenth smallest in land area. In fact, in two separate 2014 polls, viewers of ABC's *Good Morning America*, as well as readers of *USA Today*, voted Acadia number one.

Acadia is so attractive that visitation since 2007 jumped by 69 percent to 3.5 million visitors in 2017, prompting the National Park Service to launch a major effort to approve new ways to deal with frequent overcrowding and increasing traffic at the park during peak season.

In 2018 the park revealed a proposal for a possible vehicle reservation system with an additional fee for the Cadillac Summit Road, the Ocean Drive corridor, and the north lot of the Jordan Pond House from about mid-May to mid-October. If approved, the reservation system and other pos-sibilities, including phasing out right-lane parking on some one-way sections of the Park Loop Road, would go into effect for the 2020 season under a new transportation plan.

But with about 155 miles of hiking trails and 45 miles of carriage roads throughout its nearly 50,000 acres (including almost 13,000 acres under conservation easement), the park still provides plenty of opportunities for tranquility and for experiencing nature, history, geology, and culture.

This guide is for those with limited time to hike Acadia, or for those who want to sample only the easiest or most popular trails. This fourth edition of *Best Easy Day Hikes Acadia National Park* was researched as part of an update of our more comprehensive guide, *Hiking Acadia National Park*, and comes just as Acadia celebrates the hundredth anniversary of its founding as a national park.

Many of the trails described here are very easy and suitable for families with young children, but some are more challenging hikes that are among the most popular in the area, bringing you to grand mountaintop vistas. The "Trail Finder" section of this guide offers a listing of hikes by characteristic, such as "Best Hikes for Children" or "Best Hikes for Great Views."

Excluded from this guide are cliff climbs and Isle au Haut and Schoodic Peninsula trails, which are in the more comprehensive *Hiking Acadia National Park*. Also excluded: the 45 miles of carriage roads that are used by bicyclists, horseback riders, and horse-drawn carriages.

Since the first edition of this guide, new trails have been added and trail names have been changed to reflect a comprehensive multiyear, multimillion-dollar effort by the National Park Service and Acadia Trails Forever to update the historic network. The extensive system includes Native American paths, old roads, and trails built by local village improvement associations near the turn of the twentieth century, as documented by the National Park Service's Olmsted Center for Landscape Preservation.

For example, what was called the Bear Brook Trail in the first edition is now the Champlain North Ridge Trail, as already reflected on trailhead signs.

But a note of caution: In some cases the Park Service may not yet have updated trail signs—it's a multiyear process—even though the plan is to ultimately rename some of the historic trails. For that reason the old trail names are listed in this guide in parentheses for reference.

We mention Island Explorer bus stops near trailheads, if you visit during peak season (summer through fall foliage season) and want to take advantage of this increasingly popular, fare-free, and eco-friendly way of getting around Acadia. The bus driver may also make specially requested stops, if it's safe to do so. Be sure to buy a park pass to help support the Island Explorer and other programs offered by the Park Service.

Aside from hiking some of the trails described here, visitors may also want to stop at the Abbe Museum, the Wild Gardens of Acadia, and the Nature Center, all located at the Sieur de Monts entrance to the park, on ME 3 south of Bar Harbor.

The Abbe Museum, founded by Dr. Robert Abbe, a pioneer of the medical use of radium, celebrates and preserves the culture and heritage of Native Americans who lived here thousands of years before European settlers set eyes on the Maine coast. In addition to the seasonal museum at the Sieur de Monts entrance, there is a year-round museum facility in downtown Bar Harbor.

The Wild Gardens of Acadia and the Nature Center introduce the visitor to some of the flora and fauna of Acadia. The whole Sieur de Monts Spring area, especially the gardens in early morning, is an excellent bird-watching spot, with the possibility of sighting warblers, woodpeckers, flycatchers, and thrushes.

Weather

In the space of an hour or less, the weather in Acadia can change from sunny and warm to wind-whipped rain, especially on mountaintops. Summer highs average seventy to eighty degrees Fahrenheit, although fog can be common, with lows in the fifties. In the spring, highs average fifty to sixty degrees Fahrenheit, and it can be rainy. The fall brings highs in the low seventies, but rain or snow can be expected. In the winter, temperatures range from below zero to thirty degrees Fahrenheit, and snowfall averages about 60 inches a year.

Rules and Regulations

Pets must be kept on leashes no longer than 6 feet and are not allowed on ladder trails or in public water supplies. They are also prohibited on Sand Beach from June 15 up until the weekend after Labor Day, and Echo Lake from May 15 to September 15; public buildings; ranger-led programs; and the Wild Gardens of Acadia. (Service animals are an exception to these rules.) The Park Service is continually reevaluating the pet policy. Be sure to follow the rules, or you might ruin the visit for other hikers and pet owners or harm your pet and wildlife.

Parking, camping, and fires are only allowed in designated spots. No camping is allowed in the backcountry, only in Seawall Campground and Blackwoods Campground. Seawall is closed in winter. Blackwoods is open year-round but with only primitive camping from December 1 through March

31. Firearms are prohibited in the park unless they are packed away or unless other exceptions under federal and Maine law apply, such as permitted concealed carry.

Safety and Preparation

Use caution near cliffs and water's edge, especially during stormy weather. People have been swept to sea by storm-driven waves. Don't turn your back on the ocean.

Wear proper footwear, ideally hiking boots, especially for the more challenging hikes; sneakers or some other sturdy closed-toe, rubber-soled shoe may be suitable for the easiest hikes. Trails and rocks can be slippery, especially when wet. Loose gravel on rocks can also be dangerous. Most injuries come from falls while hiking or biking.

Carry at least one quart of water per person. Do not count on finding water on any hike, but if you must use natural water sources, treat with water purifiers or iodine tablets before consumption.

Wear sunscreen and protective clothing, especially a hat, to protect against the potentially harmful effects of overexposure to the sun.

Dress in layers and pack rain gear so that you are prepared for changes in weather. Bring extra socks and clothing.

If you hike alone, tell a reliable person your hiking plans, especially if you will be hiking in the more remote areas. Stick to your plan when you are on the hike, and be sure to check in upon your return.

Do not leave valuables in your car.

Day Hiker Checklist

- Day pack
- Food

- First-aid kit
- Insect repellent
- Headlamp or flashlight
- Camera
- Binoculars
- Trail guide
- Detailed trail map
- Compass or GPS unit
- Signal mirror
- Toilet paper and zippered plastic bags
- Sun hat
- Cell phone for emergencies

Leave No Trace

Many of the trails in Acadia National Park are heavily used, particularly in the peak summer months and into September. We, as trail users and advocates, must be especially vigilant to make sure our passage leaves no lasting mark.

Follow these Leave No Trace principles:

- Leave with everything you brought.
- Leave no sign of your visit.
- Leave the landscape as you found it.

And here are some additional guidelines for preserving trails in the park:

- Pack out all your own trash, including biodegradable items like orange peels. You might also pack out garbage left by less-considerate hikers.

- Don't approach or feed any wild creatures—the ground squirrel eyeing your snack food is best able to survive if it remains self-reliant. Plus it's prohibited in the park.
- Don't pick wildflowers or gather rocks, shells, and other natural or historic features along the trail. Removing these items will only take away from the next hiker's experience. Plus it's prohibited in the park.
- Don't alter the cairns, or piles of rocks that serve as trail markers, or create new ones.
- Avoid damaging trailside soils and plants by remaining on the established route.
- Walk single file in the center of the trail.
- Don't cut switchbacks, which can promote erosion.
- Be courteous by not making loud noises or casual cell phone calls while hiking.
- Many of these trails are shared with trail runners and dog walkers, and some are accessible to visitors with wheelchairs or baby strollers. Familiarize yourself with the proper trail etiquette, yielding the trail when appropriate.
- Use facilities at trailheads where available. Bury human waste in areas without toilets, and pack out toilet paper.
- Pick up after pets.

Visitor Information

Information about the park may be obtained by contacting Acadia National Park, 20 McFarland Hill Rd., PO Box 177, Bar Harbor, ME 04609-0177. The telephone number is (207) 288-3338, and the website is www.nps.gov/acad.

The Hulls Cove Visitor Center is located on ME 3, northwest of Bar Harbor. It is open from 8:30 a.m. to 4:30

p.m. daily from April 15 through June, plus September after Labor Day, and October. It is open from 8 a.m. to 6 p.m. daily from July through Labor Day. The Village Green Information Center across from the Island Explorer bus hub in Bar Harbor is open from 8 a.m. to 5 p.m. daily from mid-May through Columbus Day.

Winter visitor services are shared with the Bar Harbor Chamber of Commerce at 2 Cottage St., at the corner of Main Street, Bar Harbor. Hours are 8 a.m. to 4 p.m. daily from November through April 14.

Some hiking trails and parts of the 27-mile Park Loop Road are seasonally closed or may be closed for safety reasons or to protect nesting peregrine falcons. Check for trail and road closures with National Park Service officials or at www.nps.gov/acad.

Park entrance fees apply between May 1 and October 31, with a seven-day pass available for one vehicle; a seven-day pass for one individual on foot, motorcycle, or bicycle; and an annual pass for one vehicle.

From late June to Columbus Day, the fare-free Island Explorer bus operates between points on Mount Desert Island and the park. For schedules, routes, stops, and other information, go to exploreacadia.com.

Hikers also might find the National Geographic Acadia National Park Trails Illustrated Topographic Map helpful. You can go to www.natgeomaps.com/ti-212-acadia-national-park to get your Trails Illustrated map, or find other maps and literature at the park's visitor center.

How to Use This Guide

This guide is designed to be simple and easy to use.

Each hike is described with a map and summary information that delivers the trail's vital statistics, including length, difficulty, and canine compatibility.

Directions to the trailhead are also provided, along with a general description of what you'll see along the way. A detailed route finder ("Miles and Directions") sets forth mileage between significant landmarks along the trail.

Trailhead GPS coordinates listed in the "Finding the trailhead" section of each hike description are based on data collected by us, provided by Acadia National Park, or gathered from other reliable sources, such as the website of the US Board of Geographic Names, http://geonames.usgs.gov. If your GPS uses a different notation than the one used here, you can convert data here: http://transition.fcc.gov/mb/audio/bickel/DDDMMSS-decimal.html.

But, as with any GPS data provided for recreational use, there are no warranties, expressed or implied, about data accuracy, completeness, reliability, or suitability. The data should *not* be used for primary navigation. Readers of this guide assume the entire risk as to the quality and use of the data.

Acadia National Park officials advise that visitors obey posted signs and park regulations, pay attention to common sense, and avoid accidentally traveling on private lands while using a GPS unit.

Difficulty Ratings

These are all easy hikes, but easy is a relative term. To aid in the selection of a hike that suits particular needs and abilities, each is rated easy, moderate, or more challenging. Bear in mind that even the most challenging routes can be made easy by hiking within your limits and taking rests when you need them.

- **Easy** hikes are generally short and flat, taking no longer than 1 to 2 hours to complete.
- **Moderate** hikes involve relatively mild changes in elevation and will take 1 to 2.5 hours to complete.
- **More challenging** hikes feature some steep stretches, greater distances, and generally take longer than 2.5 hours to complete.

These are completely subjective ratings—consider that what you think is easy is entirely dependent on your level of fitness and the adequacy of your gear (primarily shoes). If you are hiking with a group, you should select a hike with a rating that's appropriate for the least fit and prepared in your party.

Approximate hiking times are based on the assumption that on flat ground, most walkers average 2 miles per hour. Adjust that rate by the steepness of the terrain and your level of fitness (subtract time if you're an aerobic animal and add time if you're hiking with kids), and you have a ballpark hiking duration. Be sure to add more time if you plan to picnic or take part in other activities like bird watching or photography.

Trail Finder

Best Hikes for Great Views

Best Hikes for Children

Best Hikes for Dogs

Map Legend

═══⟨3⟩═══	State Highway
═══════	Local Road
─ ─ ─ ─ ─	Unpaved Road
■■■■■■■	Featured Trail
- - - - -	Trail
〜〜〜	River/Creek
─·─·─	Intermittent Stream
⟋⟍	Marsh
▭	National Park
⛵	Boat Ramp
⌣	Bridge
⛺	Campground
🗼	Lighthouse
▲	Mountain/Peak
P	Parking
⊞	Picnic Area
■	Point of Interest/Structure
⊞	Restaurant
⊞	Restroom
⟋	Spring
○	Town
11	Trailhead
⌶	Tower
☎	Telephone
⚑	Viewpoint
?	Visitor/Information Center
≋	Waterfall

Mount Desert Island East of Somes Sound

Most of Acadia National Park's trails, the main Park Loop Road, and many of the best views are here on the eastern half of Mount Desert Island. Most of the "best easy" hikes are also located here.

The various hikes in this section are grouped into three geographic divisions: the Bar Harbor/Cadillac and Champlain Mountains area, the Gorham Mountain area, and the Jordan Pond and Bubbles area.

From trails in the Bar Harbor/Cadillac and Champlain Mountains area, you can get some of Acadia's best-known views of Bar Harbor, Frenchman Bay, and the Porcupine Islands. The park's Sieur de Monts entrance is also here, allowing access to the Wild Gardens of Acadia, the Nature Center, and the Abbe Museum.

The Gorham Mountain area features such seashore hikes as Sand Beach and Great Head Trail and the very easy Ocean Path, as well as such moderate hikes as the Gorham Mountain Trail.

The Quarry and Otter Cove Trails, opened in 2014, allow campers staying at Blackwoods Campground to access Gorham Mountain Trail and Ocean Path.

At the heart of the Jordan Pond and Bubbles area is the Jordan Pond House, famous for its afternoon tea and popovers and its view of the twin peaks known as the Bubbles.

The Jordan Pond House serves as a jumping-off point for an easy trail around the pond. Other dominant features accessible by trails in this area include a precariously perched rock known as Bubble Rock, and one of Acadia's famed carriage road bridges, Cobblestone Bridge.

1 Bar Island Trail

A low-tide walk leads to a rocky island off Bar Harbor, providing a unique perspective back toward town and its mountain backdrop. The trail can also offer a close-up view of gulls feeding, or starfish exposed by the tide.

Distance: 2.0 miles out and back

Approximate hiking time: 1 to 1.5 hours

Difficulty: Easy

Trail surface: Low-tide gravel bar, gravel road, forest floor, rock ledges

Best season: Spring through fall, particularly early morning or late afternoon in the summer to avoid the crowds

Other trail users: Trail runners, motorists on gravel bar

Canine compatibility: Leashed dogs permitted

Nat Geo Trails Illustrated Topographic Map: Acadia National Park

Special considerations: Accessible only 1.5 hours on either side of low tide. Check tide chart on Bar Island, in local newspapers, or at https://me.usharbors.com/monthly-tides/Maine-Downeast/Bar%20Harbor. There is a public restroom at the intersection of West and Main Streets.

Finding the trailhead: From the park's visitor center, head south on ME 3 for about 2.5 miles, toward downtown Bar Harbor. Turn left (east) onto West Street at the first intersection after the College of the Atlantic. The trail, visible only at low tide, leaves from Bridge Street, the first left (north) off West Street on the edge of downtown. There is limited on-street parking on West Street. The closest Island Explorer stop is Bar Harbor Village Green, which is available on the Campgrounds, Eden Street, Sand Beach/Blackwoods, Jordan Pond, Brown Mountain, and Southwest Harbor lines. **GPS:** N44 23.30' / W68 12.35'

The Hike

The Bar Island Trail is a short, easy jaunt within shouting distance of Bar Harbor, but you feel transported to another world. That is the beauty of being on an island, even a small one, so close to a busy summer resort town.

It's easy enough for the least-seasoned hiker, with Dolores's mother, April, a first-time visitor to Acadia at 71, effortlessly strolling across. But the Bar Island Trail also provides a bit of risk to satisfy the thrill-seeking adventurer—it can only be traveled at low tide, when a gravel bar connecting Bar Harbor and the island is exposed. The incoming tide can quickly cover the bar and prevent people from hiking off the island.

"Time your hike carefully" a sign warns hikers once they reach the island's rocky shores. "The tide changes quickly. Plan to be off the bar no later than 1.5 hours after low tide," lest you become stuck. For your convenience, a tide chart is posted, as well as phone numbers for a water taxi and Acadia dispatch if a water taxi is unavailable. Don't become one of the visitors who periodically get stranded on the island, or whose cars get swamped while parked on the gravel bar.

First described in 1867, the trail was used by the rusticators, the popular name for visitors who came to Maine for extended summer vacations during the mid- to late nineteenth century.

It was closed for a certain period, then reopened by the National Park Service in 1990 when the island was still partly privately owned. The Park Service completed ownership of the island in 2003 when it purchased 12 acres from former *NBC News* correspondent Jack Perkins and his wife, Mary Jo, who lived for thirteen years in a small home they built there.

Perkins called the island his "garden of Eden" and detailed his time there in his 2013 book, *Finding Moosewood, Finding God*. Maybe you can also discover God, or at least a sign of God, during a hike to the half-mile-long island, as we perhaps did on a cloudless early evening in September 2017, when a bald eagle hovered for a while just above our heads near the start of the wooded island.

The hike begins at the foot of Bridge Street in Bar Harbor. Be forewarned: On a sunny summer weekend day or holiday, the walk can almost become circus-like, with big crowds and passing vehicles—and maybe one or two becoming stuck in the sand. For a more tranquil coastal trek, try early morning or late afternoon on a weekday for the low-tide hike.

Walk northwest across the gravel bar, catch a view of nearby Sheep Porcupine Island and reach Bar Island at about 0.4 mile. Some of the resort town's historic summer "cottages"—really mansions—are visible along Bar Harbor's shoreline to the left (southwest) as you cross the gravel bar.

At the end of the bar, a newer sign warns people "Do not remove or stack cobbles." A violation of Leave No Trace principles, rock stacking is an annoying form of vandalism that is increasingly marring open spaces across the country, and the Park Service is attempting to prevent it.

Once you reach Bar Island, head northeast up the gravel road behind the gate. The trail soon levels off at a grassy field. At about 0.6 mile, bear left (northeast) at a trail sign pointing into the woods toward Bar Island summit. At a fork at about 0.8 mile, marked by a cairn (a pile of rocks to mark a change in trail direction), bear right (southeast) up a rocky knob.

At about 1.0 mile you reach the summit, with its views toward Bar Harbor, as well as several Acadia peaks: from left

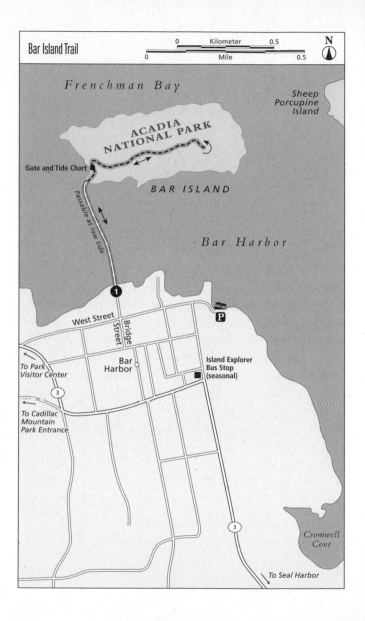

Bar Island Trail

Frenchman Bay

Sheep Porcupine Island

ACADIA NATIONAL PARK

Gate and Tide Chart

BAR ISLAND

passable at low tide

Bar Harbor

1

West Street

Bridge Street

P

To Park Visitor Center

Bar Harbor

Island Explorer Bus Stop (seasonal)

3

To Cadillac Mountain Park Entrance

3

Cromwell Cove

To Seal Harbor

Kilometer

Mile

N

to right, Champlain Mountain, Huguenot Head, and Dorr and Cadillac Mountains. From here you can hear the town's church bells, see the fishing and recreational boats along the harbor, and take in the smells of the sea and the views of the mountains.

Return the way you came.

Miles and Directions

0.0 Start at the Bar Island trailhead, at the foot of Bridge Street.

0.4 Reach the shore of Bar Island. Check the posted tide chart to time your return; otherwise you'll have to wait more than 12 hours for the next low tide. Head northeast up the gravel road behind the gate.

0.6 Cross a grassy field and come to a junction; bear left (northeast) into the woods at the trail sign.

0.8 Reach another junction marked by a cairn; bear right (southeast) up to the island's summit.

1.0 Reach the island's summit, with views back toward Bar Harbor and the mountains.

2.0 Arrive back at the trailhead.

2 Great Meadow Loop and Jesup Path to Sieur de Monts

This woods, wetlands, and field walk takes you to Sieur de Monts Spring and the newly rehabilitated Spring Pool, the Wild Gardens of Acadia, the Nature Center, and the Abbe Museum. You'll hear birdsong and get open views of Huguenot Head and the Champlain and Dorr Mountains along Great Meadow. And you can re-create the historic experience of walking between Bar Harbor and the park, like the residents and visitors of yore.

Distance: 4.2 miles out and back, or 2.1 miles one way if you take the Island Explorer back to Bar Harbor Village Green

Approximate hiking time: 2 to 3 hours

Difficulty: Easy

Trail surface: Forest floor, graded gravel path, wooden boardwalk and bridges

Best season: Spring through fall, particularly early morning or late afternoon in the summer to avoid the crowds

Other trail users: Dog walkers, trail runners, area residents

Canine compatibility: Leashed dogs permitted (but not in the Wild Gardens of Acadia, Nature Center, or Abbe Museum)

Nat Geo Trails Illustrated Topographic Map: Acadia National Park

Special considerations: Graded gravel and wooden boardwalk surfaces make part of the walk wheelchair and baby-stroller accessible. Seasonal restrooms are at the ball fields and Sieur de Monts parking area.

Finding the trailhead: From downtown Bar Harbor head south on ME 3 for about half a mile, turn right (west) onto Park Street, and park by the ball fields. Walk west on Park Street to begin the hike. The closest Island Explorer stop is Bar Harbor Village Green. During peak season you can reduce the hiking distance in half, by taking the Island Explorer at Sieur de Monts on the return. **GPS:** N44 22.58' / W68 12.11'

The Hike

This walk from Bar Harbor to Sieur de Monts, the historic heart of Acadia, may very well be one of the best hikes to mark Acadia's hundredth anniversary of its founding as a national park.

The Great Meadow Loop, partly on park land and partly on private property, is just one of the village connector trails re-created as part of the $13 million Acadia Trails Forever initiative, a joint effort of the Friends of Acadia and the National Park Service.

The idea: to provide options for walking between town and the mountains, ponds, and sea, as was the case during the days of the nineteenth- and early twentieth-century rustica-tors, or artists, tourists, and summer residents, who would think nothing of walking 5, 10, or 15 miles in a day.

First created about one hundred years ago by George B. Dorr and others as part of a garden path that connected to downtown Bar Harbor, Jesup Path connects the Great Meadow Loop to Sieur de Monts. And Sieur de Monts is where Acadia all began in 1916 as a national monument, with Dorr as its first superintendent.

The hike described here begins by the Bar Harbor ball fields and could just as easily be done in reverse, starting at the easy-to-reach Sieur de Monts parking area. But park officials encourage visitors to walk south from Bar Harbor as the rusticators did, especially during the peak summer season.

From the ball fields, walk west on Park Street, turn left (south) onto Ledgelawn Avenue, and follow it for 0.4 mile as it crosses over Cromwell Harbor Road by the former public works yard and becomes Great Meadow Drive. Turn right at a wooden bridge on the right (west) and turn quickly left (south) onto the Great Meadow Loop as it circles around Kebo Valley Golf Course. Follow the trail south for 0.4 mile as it meanders through the woods and crosses Great Meadow Drive a couple of times. As it nears the Park Loop Road, the trail bears right (west) to parallel the Park Loop Road for 0.3 mile.

Just before the Great Meadow Loop reaches a junction with Kebo Street and turns away from the Park Loop Road, cross to the left (south) over the one-way Park Loop Road (watch for traffic on the right) to pick up Jesup Path. This well-graded path takes you by the Great Meadow, across Hemlock Path a couple of times, on the way to Sieur de Monts.

You'll find plenty of birds and flowering plants along the marshy "meadow," especially in spring. As you head south on Jesup Path, look across the Great Meadow toward the Sieur de Monts area and you'll find open views of Huguenot Head and Champlain Mountain to the east (left) and Dorr Mountain to the west (right).

At the end of Jesup Path's long boardwalk, cross over Hemlock Path and head straight toward Sieur de Monts. Here you will find a rock inscribed with the words "Sweet Waters of Acadia" near the Sieur de Monts Spring House built by Dorr in 1909. You'll also find a Dorr memorial plaque.

Over the last several years, with Acadia's hundredth anniversary in mind, officials have worked toward rehabilitating the Spring Pool to Dorr's original landscaped vision. They've removed invasive plants, reset large stones, and replaced the spring-fed pool's gravel to better support spawning native brook trout.

The Spring Pool is a fitting place to reflect on Acadia's one hundred years and George Dorr, on all the park has meant for generations past, and on what it can mean for generations to come.

Return the way you came for a 4.2-mile round-trip, or catch the Island Explorer in season to your next destination.

Miles and Directions

0.0 Start at Park Street and head west, with the Bar Harbor ball fields on your left.

0.2 Turn left onto Ledgelawn Avenue.

0.3 Cross over Cromwell Harbor Road and stay straight as Ledgelawn becomes Great Meadow Drive.

0.6 Turn right (west) across a wooden bridge and quickly left (south) to follow Great Meadow Loop as it circles Kebo Valley Golf Course and crosses Great Meadow Drive a couple of times on its way toward the Park Loop Road.

1.0 Follow Great Meadow Loop right (west) as it parallels the Park Loop Road.

1.3 Just before the Great Meadow Loop reaches the junction with Kebo Street, cross left (south) over the one-way Park Loop Road (watch for traffic on the right) to pick up Jesup Path on the other side. Head straight (south) on Jesup Path.

1.6 Cross over Hemlock Path.

2.0 At the end of the long boardwalk, cross over Hemlock Path again and continue straight (southeast) on Jesup Path.

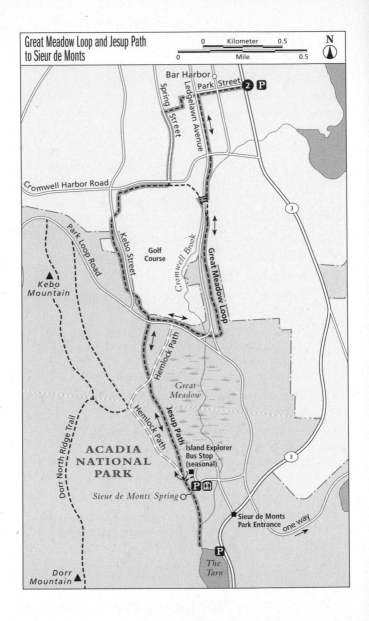

Great Meadow Loop and Jesup Path
to Sieur de Monts

Kilometer
0   0.5

Mile
0   0.5

N

Bar Harbor
Park Street   2   P
Spring Street
Ledgelawn Avenue

Cromwell Harbor Road

3

Kebo Street
Golf Course
Cromwell Brook
Great Meadow Loop

Park Loop Road

Kebo Mountain

Hemlock Path
Great Meadow

Hemlock Path
Jesup Path

Dorr North Ridge Trail

ACADIA NATIONAL PARK

Island Explorer Bus Stop (seasonal)

P

Sieur de Monts Spring

Sieur de Monts Park Entrance   one way

3

P

The Tarn

Dorr Mountain

2.1 Reach Sieur de Monts. Instead of retracing your steps, you can take the Island Explorer bus in season on the return, or explore other hiking options.

4.2 Arrive back at the trailhead.

Options

To add a 0.3-mile spur to the Tarn, head south from Sieur de Monts Spring on Jesup Path toward that glacially carved pond at the base of Dorr Mountain. A plaque at this end of the trail reads "In Memory of Morris K. and Maria DeWitt Jesup, Lovers of this Island, 1918."

Or create a loop on the return. At Jesup Path's end at the Park Loop Road, cross over the road to pick up Great Meadow Loop and turn left (west) as it heads toward and crosses Kebo Street. Follow Great Meadow Loop north 0.5 mile to Cromwell Harbor Road and turn right to parallel the road. In 0.3 mile cross over Cromwell Harbor Road to pick up Spring Street. Follow Spring Street north for 0.2 mile. Turn right (east) onto Norris Avenue, then left (north) onto Glen Mary Road, then right (east) onto Park Street to return to the start.

3 Compass Harbor Trail

Situated just outside Bar Harbor, this easy trail offers both important history—it's the former site of park pioneer George B. Dorr's Oldfarm estate—and sweeping ocean and island views—its point is right on Frenchman Bay. The trail features some remnants of Dorr's family home, older growth trees, Dorr Point, and sights along the bay.

Distance: 0.8 mile out and back

Approximate hiking time: 30 minutes

Difficulty: Easy

Trail surface: Gravel road, forest floor, sandy trail at end

Best season: Spring through fall, particularly off-peak times

Other trail users: Dog walkers, trail runners, area residents

Canine compatibility: Leashed dogs permitted

Nat Geo Trails Illustrated Topographic Map: Acadia National Park

Special considerations: No facilities. An Oldfarm app, produced by the park and Northern Arizona University to educate visitors, is used with an Apple device in tandem with 11 numbered stations along the trail.

Finding the trailhead: From downtown Bar Harbor head south on ME 3 for 1.0 mile. A small parking lot is located on the left (east) just after Nannau Wood, a private road, and just before Old Farm Road, also private. The trail begins off the parking lot. If the parking lot is full, often the case during peak times, you can park at the town ball fields and walk south just over 0.5 mile along ME 3 to the trailhead. The Island Explorer bus does not have a stop here, although the Sand Beach line goes by, and you may be able to ask the bus driver to let you off if it is safe to do so. **GPS:** N44 22.25' / W68 11.51'

The Hike

At Compass Harbor, you can see where the park's first superintendent, George B. Dorr, took his daily swim in the cold waters of Frenchman Bay or tended to the wide-ranging gardens that once surrounded his sprawling estate here called Oldfarm. The trail begins as a wide gravel road off the parking lot and soon comes to a sign pointing to Compass Harbor. The trail goes left and narrows as it approaches the ocean.

During a hike in 2018, Ranger Maureen Fournier, an authority on Compass Harbor, noted that the trail partly utilizes a road bed from a formal driveway to the mansion, which she said was considered the first well-built estate in Bar Harbor.

"Imagine going back in time one hundred years to see what this was like," said Fournier, who once conducted the park's interpretive program at Compass Harbor.

Head out on a sandy trail on a peninsula toward Dorr Point, but stop before an eroded section of the trail. Compass Harbor and Ogden Point are located to the left (north and northwest), and Sols Cliff is to the right (southeast). Frenchman Bay is straight ahead.

Near the point, look for some old granite blocks that were once part of Dorr's saltwater bathing pool that filled at high tide.

Just before reaching the point, an unofficial trail leads to the ruins of the Dorr manor house, which was built from 1880 to 1881 on land purchased by his father in 1868 and donated to the Park Service by Dorr in 1942.

We counted forty-three granite steps and came upon an aged foundation for the Oldfarm manor house and a brick patio.

"It is widely believed this is granite from his own quarry," which was owned by the family and located at the southern end of the estate, Fournier said. "The steps all come from his quarry."

In 2016, the Park Service completed a 145-page *Cultural Landscape Inventory and Assessment for Oldfarm*, which recommends management approaches for the 58 acres the park still owns from the original 100-acre estate at Compass Harbor and analyzes the historical significance of the property.

None of Dorr's formal gardens remain, but several plants and shrubs from the historic period can still be found at the manor site, Fournier said, including a large lilac and a prominent vine.

An arborvitae hedge, which likely separated a tennis court from the cutting garden, has deteriorated, but about ten to twelve trees still exist, the Park Service assessment said.

Dorr was adamant that his cherished Oldfarm become part of the park and even offered the property as a summer White House to President Calvin Coolidge in 1928 and then to the executive branch under President Franklin D. Roosevelt in 1940 to garner support, according to the assessment.

Roosevelt suggested it should be donated to the National Park Service, and the property finally became part of the park two years before Dorr died at Oldfarm. But in 1951, the Park Service found it too expensive to preserve and maintain, razing the estate, Fournier said.

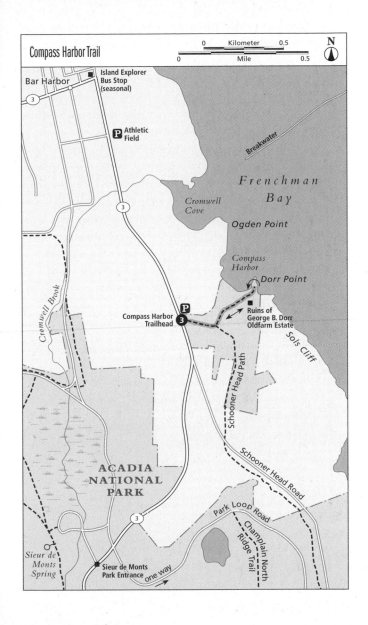

Compass Harbor Trail

0 Kilometer **0.5**

0 Mile **0.5**

N

Bar Harbor

Island Explorer
Bus Stop
(seasonal)

3

P Athletic
Field

3

Cromwell
Cove

F r e n c h m a n
B a y

Breakwater

Ogden Point

Compass
Harbor

Dorr Point

P
Compass Harbor
Trailhead
3

Ruins of
George B. Dorr
Oldfarm Estate

Cromwell Brook

Schooner Head Path

Sols Cliff

ACADIA
NATIONAL
PARK

Schooner Head Road

3

Park Loop Road

Champlain North
Ridge Trail

Sieur de
Monts
Spring

Sieur de Monts
Park Entrance   one way

"People are aghast when you tell them what happened with the house, but it was 1951, and the Park Service had no money," she explained.

At that time in the nation's history, in the wake of the Great Depression and World War II, one can imagine that the federal government didn't have the funds to keep up Oldfarm, or many other facilities or programs.

The estate's 1879 Storm Beach Cottage, where Dorr often stayed, is still in good condition and used as park staff housing.

Today the National Park Service calls Dorr the father of the park and credits him for his indefatigable work in leading the effort to create Acadia. There's no better spot to ponder that than Compass Harbor.

Return the way you came.

Miles and Directions

0.0 Start at the Compass Harbor trailhead, which leaves from the parking lot on the left (east) side of ME 3, just south of Nannau Wood, a private road.

0.1 Turn left at the junction toward Compass Harbor.

0.4 Approach Dorr Point and the remains of George B. Dorr's Oldfarm estate.

0.8 Arrive back at the trailhead.

4 Cadillac Summit Loop Trail

Located at the top of Acadia's highest mountain, this short and easy trail offers maybe the best views in the park and wayside exhibits that identify more than forty islands, peaks, and other key points that lie off its slopes. On a sunny day this loop is the best place for any hiker to get some bearings before exploring the rest of Acadia. The trail is often busy during peak summer months, since cars and buses can drive up the mountain's access road.

Distance: 0.5-mile loop
Approximate hiking time: 30 minutes
Difficulty: Easy
Trail surface: Paved walkway
Best season: Spring through fall, particularly early morning or late afternoon in the summer to avoid the crowds
Other trail users: Hikers coming from Gorge Path or Cadillac North Ridge or Cadillac South Ridge Trails, visitors with wheelchairs or baby strollers, birders

Canine compatibility: Leashed dogs permitted
Nat Geo Trails Illustrated Topographic Map: Acadia National Park
Special considerations: The walkway is partially accessible for visitors with wheelchairs or baby strollers, just the short distance from the parking lot to a viewing platform. The 3.5-mile paved auto road to the summit is a winding and narrow route. There is a seasonal summit gift shop and restrooms.

Finding the trailhead: From the park's visitor center, drive south on the Park Loop Road for about 3.5 miles and turn left (east) at the sign for Cadillac Mountain. Ascend the winding summit road to the top. The paved walkway begins off the eastern side of the parking lot, across from the summit gift shop. The Island Explorer bus does not go up Cadillac, but the Loop Road line has a Cadillac North Ridge stop, where the 2.2-mile moderately difficult Cadillac North Ridge Trail takes you to the top and a connection with the Cadillac Summit Loop Trail. **GPS:** N44 21.09' / W68 13.28'

The Hike

You gain a new appreciation for 1,530-foot-high Cadillac Mountain on this trail, with wayside exhibits describing the history and features of Mount Desert Island and the panoramic views from the highest point on the East Coast of the United States.

The 0.5-mile summit loop trail on the peak includes two viewing platforms and excellent vistas of the Porcupine and Cranberry Islands, Frenchman Bay, Great Head, the Beehive, Otter Point, and Dorr and other mountains.

Near the start of the trail off the parking lot, a bronze memorial plaque, installed in 1932, commemorates Stephen Tyng Mather, a wealthy entrepreneur, leading advocate for the creation of the National Park Service in 1916, and its first director.

Newly designed wayside exhibits, erected in 2015 along the trail and the edge of the parking lot, describe significant aspects of the area, including the geological essence of Acadia—the pink granite with its three main minerals; the night sky over Acadia; and the visionaries who helped found the park a century ago, from George B. Dorr to Charles Eliot and John D. Rockefeller Jr.

A top feature of this hike is a circular platform with two exhibits that pinpoint about forty highlights of the sweeping views, allowing anyone to find spots such as Turtle Island, Egg Rock, Schoodic Point, Porcupine Islands, Seawall

Campground, Baker Island, Little Cranberry Island, and the Gulf of Maine.

Aside from the islands and other sites, you may also hear song sparrows during the spring, or see bald eagles and turkey vultures soaring above Cadillac, especially during the annual HawkWatch from late August through mid-October, when migrating raptors such as kestrels, peregrine falcons, and sharp-shinned hawks can be spotted.

You may also see three-toothed cinquefoil, lowbush blueberries, a tiny white flower known as mountain sandwort, and the pink blooms of rhodora. Even a couple of small birch trees can be found along the walkway, proof of the success of restoration efforts over the past decade or so. Wooden barricades and signs reminding hikers to stay on the trail and solid rock are part of the continued revegetation program in the wake of uncontrolled trampling in the past that caused erosion and changed the appearance of the area.

Don't look for a peak sign off the trail. The peak of Cadillac, as marked by the US Geological Survey, is actually off the Cadillac South Ridge Trail, near an antenna behind the gift shop, but the best views are from the loop trail.

There are two access points to the paved summit loop trail off the eastern edge of the parking area. The access point on the left (northeast), near the handicapped parking spots, is also the start of a 2005 paved path that can be used by physically disabled persons and people with baby strollers to reach the main viewing platform without climbing stairs.

The trail, started by the Park Service in 1932 and completed the following year by the Civilian Conservation Corps—the Depression-era public work relief program—is tinged to match the pink Cadillac granite and features several sets of granite boulders for steps. Even though the trail is

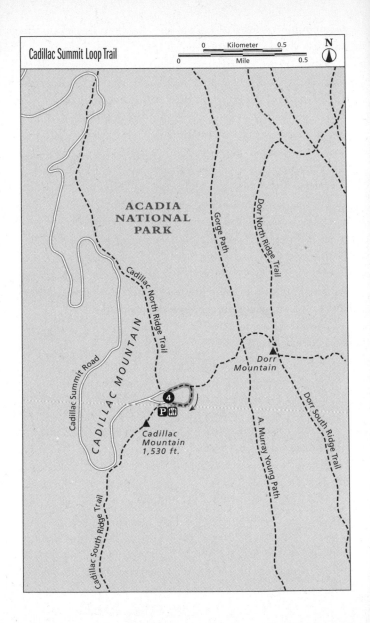

easy, watch your footing; people have been injured along the walkway, which can be uneven in spots.

The road to the summit, finished in 1932 by the Park Service, was among the first motor roads built in the park. Before the road was built, an entrepreneur constructed a cog railway in 1883 to the peak from Eagle Lake, but it was dismantled ten years later because people generally preferred to escape the industrial age by hiking or taking a horse-drawn buckboard to the peak.

Because of its grand vistas and easy access, the trail can get very crowded in the summer. Early and late in the day are best. But there can be small crowds even before dawn to catch the sunrise, which can be magnificent on Cadillac, the first place in the United States where the sun's rays hit between October 7 and March 6, generally. And there can even be a motor brigade heading up for the sunset, as we have found on many days as dusk approached.

Miles and Directions

0.0   Start at the Cadillac Summit Loop trailhead, with two access points located at the eastern edge of the parking area, across from the summit shop. The left (northeastern) trail entrance connects to a ramp that allows wheelchair and baby stroller access to a circular viewing area.

0.5   Complete the loop back at the trailhead.

5 Beachcroft Path

Intricately laid stone steps lead much of the way to open views along Huguenot Head, on the shoulder of Champlain Mountain. In line with its more-than-a-century-old history, this route's name is reverting to the original description as a path, rather than a trail, to better characterize its highly constructed nature. It's a mostly moderate ascent to this hike's goal, but there's an option to climb more strenuously for another 0.5 mile to reach the summit of Champlain and its ocean views.

Distance: 1.4 miles out and back

Approximate hiking time: 1 to 1.5 hours

Difficulty: Moderate to more challenging

Trail surface: Granite steps, rock ledges, forest floor

Best season: Spring through fall

Other trail users: None

Canine compatibility: Leashed dogs permitted

Nat Geo Trails Illustrated Topographic Map: Acadia National Park

Special considerations: If you tack on the stretch to the top of Champlain, be aware that the steep section is not recommended for dogs. There are no facilities at the trailhead. Seasonal restrooms are at the nearby Sieur de Monts park entrance.

Finding the trailhead: From downtown Bar Harbor head south on ME 3 for about 2.2 miles, just past the park's Sieur de Monts entrance, to the parking lot on the right (west) just before the glacially carved lake known as the Tarn. The trailhead is on the left (east) side of ME 3, across the road diagonally (southeast) from the parking lot. Be careful crossing ME 3. The closest Island Explorer stop is Sieur de Monts on the Sand Beach and Loop Road lines. **GPS:** N44 21.30' / W68 12.19'

The Hike

The Beachcroft Path climbs to the shoulder of Huguenot Head, with an average elevation gain of 100 feet each tenth of a mile, but at times it feels remarkably like a walk along a garden path. The gradual switchbacks and neatly laid stepping-stones turn what would otherwise be a vertical scramble into a gentler ascent.

Adding to the wonder are the constant open views toward Frenchman Bay, Dorr Mountain, the Cranberry Isles, Champlain Mountain, and the Tarn.

The dome-shaped Huguenot Head, visible from Bar Harbor, has been a popular destination for more than a century. The Beachcroft Path, built and rebuilt in the late 1800s and early 1900s, was named for the estate of the Bar Harbor summer resident who financed its construction. It consists of hundreds of hand-hewn stepping-stones and countless switchbacks. When it was originally constructed by George B. Dorr and the Bar Harbor Village Improvement Association, the path began at Sieur de Monts Spring, but the path's start later had to be moved because of road construction.

From the trailhead across from the Tarn parking area, ascend via the switchbacks and stone steps, catching your breath on the plentiful level sections along the way. But be careful, as even the flattest-looking rock along the path can be loose, and watch your step as you travel on open rock ledges.

Near the shoulder of Huguenot Head, the path widens and levels off. It circles to the northeast as you reach the open ledge just below the head's summit, ending at 0.7 mile with views south toward the Cranberry Isles. To the east (left) is Champlain Mountain, and to the west (right) is Dorr Mountain. Down below are the Tarn and ME 3.

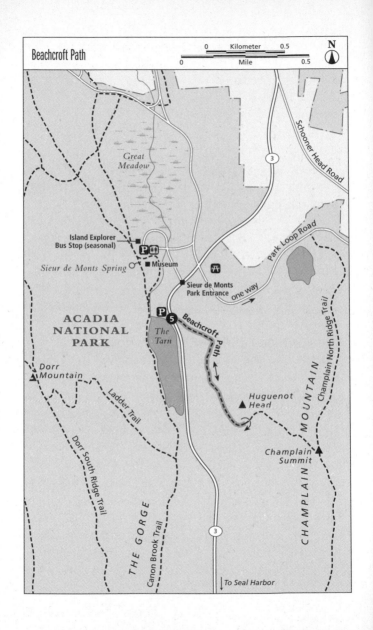

Beachcroft Path

Kilometer
0   0.5
0   0.5
Mile

N

Great
Meadow

Island Explorer
Bus Stop (seasonal)

Sieur de Monts Spring

Museum

Sieur de Monts
Park Entrance

one way

Park Loop Road

Schooner Head Road

3

ACADIA
NATIONAL
PARK

The
Tarn

Beachcroft Path

Dorr
Mountain

Ladder Trail

Huguenot
Head

Champlain North Ridge Trail

CHAMPLAIN   MOUNTAIN

Champlain
Summit

Dorr South Ridge Trail

THE GORGE

Canon Brook Trail

3

To Seal Harbor

Return the way you came. Ambitious hikers can continue east toward the summit of Champlain Mountain, a more challenging additional 0.5-mile climb.

Miles and Directions

0.0 Start at the Beachcroft Path trailhead, diagonally (southeast) across ME 3 from the parking lot that's just south of the Sieur de Monts park entrance.

0.7 Reach the open ledge on the shoulder of Huguenot Head and enjoy the views.

1.4 Arrive back at the trailhead.

6 Champlain North Ridge Trail (Bear Brook Trail)

Enjoy expansive views from the summit of Champlain Mountain and all along the open ridge, the closest to the ocean of all of Acadia's ridges. At times you'll see the contrast of fog rolling in over Frenchman Bay below and sun shining overhead, or storm clouds streaming in from the west as clear skies still prevail to the east.

Distance: 2.0 miles out and back

Approximate hiking time: 1.5 to 2 hours

Difficulty: Moderate to more challenging

Trail surface: Rock ledges, forest floor

Best season: Spring through fall

Other trail users: None

Canine compatibility: Leashed dogs permitted

Nat Geo Trails Illustrated Topographic Map: Acadia National Park

Special considerations: No facilities at trailhead; seasonal restrooms at nearby Bear Brook picnic area

Finding the trailhead: Enter the park at the Sieur de Monts entrance, which is about 2 miles south of downtown Bar Harbor on ME 3. Turn right (south) onto the one-way Park Loop Road. The trailhead is 0.8 mile from the entrance, on the right (south) after the Bear Brook picnic area. There is a small parking area on the left (north), across the road just beyond the trailhead. The closest Island Explorer stop is Sieur de Monts on the Loop Road and Sand Beach lines, but it's a bit of a walk, so you may want to ask if the bus driver can let you off at the trailhead. **GPS:** N44 21.47' / W68 11.36'

The Hike

On the Champlain North Ridge Trail early one morning, a blanket of fog rolled in and enveloped the Porcupine Islands in the space of a few minutes. Amazingly, the ridgetop trail continued to be bathed in sunshine as the foghorns sounded their warnings below.

Another time, we started a late afternoon walk under sunny skies, but by the time we got to the summit a mile away, strong rain forced us to put on full storm gear from head to toe. It was sunny once again as we returned to the trailhead.

Contrasts like these are part of the very nature of Acadia, where the mountains meet the sea and the weather can vary from moment to moment.

The trail, recently renamed as part of a multiyear effort to update some of the park's historic routes, offers spectacular views from Frenchman Bay to Great Head as it climbs the northern ridge of 1,058-foot Champlain Mountain. This is one of the oldest marked trails on Mount Desert Island, showing up on 1890s maps, when Champlain used to be known as Newport Mountain.

From the trailhead head south and start ascending through a birch grove. The trail levels off a bit at about 0.2 mile and then ascends more steeply up some stone steps.

The junction with the Orange & Black Path (formerly known as the East Face Trail) is at 0.4 mile. Continue straight (south) and climb a steep pink-granite face. Follow blue blazes and Bates-style cairns (artfully placed groups of four to six rocks that point the way) as you near the summit.

As part of staying true to the history of Acadia's trails, the Bates cairns, pioneered by Waldron Bates, chair of the Roads

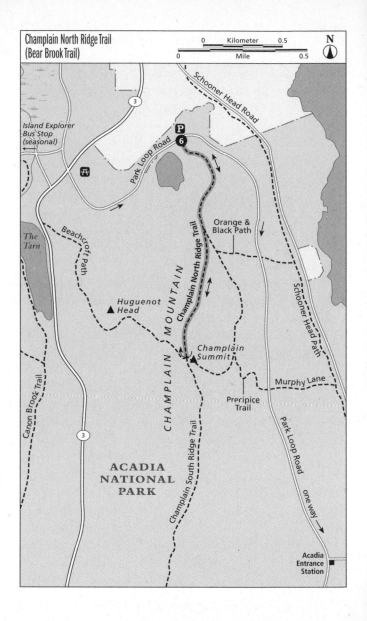

Champlain North Ridge Trail (Bear Brook Trail)

0   Kilometer   0.5

0   Mile   0.5

N

Schooner Head Road

3

Island Explorer
Bus Stop
(seasonal)

Park Loop Road

P
6

Orange &
Black Path

Beachcroft Path

The Tarn

Huguenot Head

Champlain North Ridge Trail

CHAMPLAIN MOUNTAIN

Champlain Summit

Murphy Lane

Preripice Trail

Schooner Head Path

Canon Brook Trail

3

Champlain South Ridge Trail

ACADIA
NATIONAL
PARK

Park Loop Road

one way

Acadia
Entrance
Station

and Paths Committee of the Bar Harbor Village Improvement Association from 1900 to 1909, have replaced conical piles of rocks and supplement blue blazes as trail markers, particularly on ridgelines on the east side of Mount Desert Island. Don't be tempted to move, add, or take away rocks from the seemingly Zen-like Bates cairns. They are designed with a purpose, with the gap in the base and the top stone pointing in the right direction. Any alteration can wreak havoc for other hikers, never mind for those maintaining the trails.

At 1.0 mile reach the Champlain summit, with the closest mountaintop views of Frenchman Bay and the Porcupine Islands in all of Acadia. You also reach the junction with the Precipice and Champlain South Ridge Trails and the upper Beachcroft Path at the summit.

Return the way you came. Intrepid hikers can continue down the Champlain South Ridge Trail for another 1.6 miles to a mountain pond known as the Bowl.

Miles and Directions

0.0   Start at the Champlain North Ridge trailhead, on the right (south) side of the one-way Park Loop Road, after the Bear Brook picnic area.

0.4   Reach the junction with the Orange & Black Path. Continue straight on the main trail.

1.0   Arrive at the Champlain Mountain summit and the junction with the Precipice and Champlain South Ridge Trails and the upper Beachcroft Path.

2.0   Arrive back at the trailhead.

7 Schooner Head Overlook and Path

Sample a unique Acadia experience by walking along recently reopened historic trails from a spectacular shore overlook to the base of Champlain's cliffs, with options for longer treks. Along the way you'll pass through deciduous forest and by grand cliff views, and you can imagine what it was like when nineteenth-century rusticators traveled these same footpaths.

Distance: 2.0 miles out and back

Approximate hiking time: 1 to 1.5 hours

Difficulty: Easy

Trail surface: Forest floor, graded gravel path, wooden bridge

Best season: Spring through fall

Other trail users: Trail runners, dog walkers, area residents

Canine compatibility: Leashed dogs permitted

Nat Geo Trails Illustrated Topographic Map: Acadia National Park

Special considerations: No facilities at trailhead

Finding the trailhead: From the park's visitor center, drive south on the Park Loop Road for about 3 miles and turn left (east) at the sign for Sand Beach. Follow the one-way Park Loop Road for about 5 miles. Turn left (east) just before the park entrance station and head straight 0.2 mile, across Schooner Head Road, to the Schooner Head Overlook parking lot. The trailhead is at the northwest corner of the parking lot, before the exit to Schooner Head Road. There is no nearby Island Explorer stop, but the Sand Beach and Loop Road lines pass through the nearby park entrance station, and you may ask the bus driver to let you off there if it is safe to do so. **GPS:** N44 20.22' / W68 10.44'

The Hike

Where else but in Acadia can you go from shore to cliff in just a mile? And also step through time?

Start off by taking in the oceanfront views at Schooner Head Overlook, at the easternmost end of the parking lot. To the north (left) is the rocky peninsula known as Schooner Head, and out in Frenchman Bay is Egg Rock, with its lighthouse. And as of 2014, with the clearing of trees and restoration of historic vistas, the precipice of Champlain Mountain is visible to the northwest once again.

Head to the northwest corner of the parking lot and pick up Schooner Head Path, a recently reopened historic route. While the hike described here is along only a portion of Schooner Head Path, you can still imagine yourself a modern-day rusticator, seeing some of the same views that Hudson River School artists like Thomas Cole and Frederic Church saw, or that George B. Dorr, regarded as the father of Acadia, fought so hard to protect. The path, first built in 1901, recently reopened with funds from the Acadia Trails Forever initiative and the private Fore River Foundation, and is a cooperative effort of the Park Service, Friends of Acadia, area residents, the town of Bar Harbor, and nearby Jackson Laboratory.

Follow the well-graded and slightly hilly path through the woods for 0.1 mile, then cross Schooner Head Road and pick up the trail as it continues on the other side. The path eventually levels off and parallels Schooner Head Road, taking you over a wooden bridge built over the outlet of a pond at 0.2 mile. Take in the grand views of the Champlain cliffs, your destination on this hike.

At 0.7 mile turn left (west) onto Murphy Lane, another recently reopened historic trail that was once open to horses and known as the Blue Path, showing up on maps dating back to the 1890s. Follow Murphy Lane straight (west) through the woods, and don't be confused by old trails that may crisscross in spots.

At 1.0 mile cross the one-way Park Loop Road (look right for traffic) and arrive at the base of Champlain's cliffs, at the Precipice parking area. The Precipice Trail begins here, but it is one of the most difficult cliff climbs in Acadia and not suitable for novices or people afraid of heights. If the trail is closed for peregrine falcon nesting season, you can participate in a peregrine watch with park rangers and volunteers who set up spotting scopes in the Precipice parking area.

Return the way you came.

Miles and Directions

0.0 Start at the Schooner Head Path trailhead, in the northwest corner of the Schooner Head Overlook parking lot, before the exit to Schooner Head Road.

0.1 Cross Schooner Head Road and continue on the path on the other (west) side of the road.

0.2 Cross a wooden bridge over the outlet of a pond, with views toward the Champlain cliffs.

0.7 Reach a junction with Murphy Lane. Turn left (west) and stay straight on the woods trail.

1.0 Cross the one-way Park Loop Road (look right for traffic) to reach the base of the Champlain cliffs at the Precipice parking area. Participate in a peregrine watch if it's peregrine falcon nesting season.

2.0 Arrive back at the trailhead.

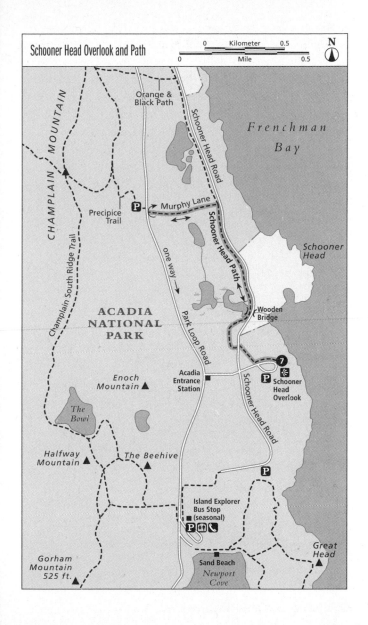

Schooner Head Overlook and Path

0   Kilometer   0.5
0   Mile   0.5

N

CHAMPLAIN MOUNTAIN

Orange & Black Path

Schooner Head Road

Frenchman Bay

Murphy Lane

Precipice Trail

Champlain South Ridge Trail

one way

Schooner Head Path

Schooner Head

ACADIA NATIONAL PARK

Wooden Bridge

Enoch Mountain

Park Loop Road

Acadia Entrance Station

7

Schooner Head Overlook

Schooner Head Road

The Bowl

Halfway Mountain

The Beehive

Island Explorer Bus Stop (seasonal)

Gorham Mountain 525 ft.

Sand Beach

Newport Cove

Great Head

Options

To explore more of Schooner Head Path, instead of turning left on Murphy Lane, continue straight (north) on the well-graded path as it parallels Schooner Head Road. In another 0.5 mile you reach a junction with the Orange & Black Path on the left (west), a more difficult trail that leads up Champlain's east face and connects to the Champlain North Ridge and Precipice Trails. Beyond that junction, Schooner Head Path continues another 1.6 miles northwest and then north by northeast all the way to Compass Harbor on the outskirts of Bar Harbor. Some parts of the northern section of Schooner Head Path cross private property, so be respectful of property owners' rights and stay on the established route.

8 Sand Beach and Great Head Trail

Enjoy Acadia's only ocean beach, made of sand, tiny shell fragments, quartz, and pink feldspar. Then take a hike along the Great Head Trail for its expansive views of the Beehive, Champlain Mountain, Otter Cliff, Egg Rock, and the Cranberry Isles. Also visible just off the tip of Great Head peninsula is an unusual rock formation called Old Soaker.

Distance: 1.7-mile lollipop
Approximate hiking time: 1 to 1.5 hours
Difficulty: Moderate
Trail surface: Beach, rock ledges, forest floor
Best season: Spring through fall, particularly early morning or late afternoon in the summer to avoid the beach crowds
Other trail users: Sunbathers on Sand Beach in summertime
Canine compatibility: Dogs prohibited on Sand Beach from June 15 through the weekend after Labor Day; leashed dogs permitted other times of year
Nat Geo Trails Illustrated Topographic Map: Acadia National Park
Special considerations: Seasonal restrooms and changing area are available at the Sand Beach parking lot; bring extra socks or a towel in case your feet get wet when you cross a small channel to get from the beach to the trailhead.

Finding the trailhead: From the park's visitor center, drive south on the Park Loop Road for about 3 miles and turn left (east) at the sign for Sand Beach. Follow the one-way Park Loop Road for about 5.5 miles, past the park entrance station, to the beach parking lot on the left (east) side of the road. The Island Explorer's Loop Road and Sand Beach lines stop at the beach parking lot. Walk down the stairs at the eastern end of the parking lot and head east across Sand Beach to the Great Head trailhead. **GPS:** N44 19.45' / W68 11.01'

The Hike

A hike on the Great Head peninsula is a perfect way to break up a lazy summer afternoon lounging on Sand Beach. Because it is so quintessentially Acadia, it's also a perfect place to bring first-time visitors, as we have with our nieces Sharon, Michelle, and Stacey.

A relatively modest scramble up the rocky slope of Great Head leads to dramatic views of the beach you just left behind, as well as vistas of such other notable park features as the Beehive, Champlain Mountain, and Otter Cliff.

Once, when we hiked Great Head with Sharon and Michelle, the views were made even more dramatic by the fog that first enveloped Sand Beach and the Beehive behind us, and then receded like the outgoing tide.

"I feel like I'm living in a postcard," said Sharon, fifteen at the time.

"This is really fun," said Michelle, twelve at the time, as opposed to the "kind of fun" rating she gave to a hike with less dramatic views the day before.

Since the 1840s and 1850s, Great Head has been a popular destination for artists and tourists. A stone teahouse, known as Satterlee's Tower, once stood on the summit, and the ruins of it are still visible.

Once, as we stood by the ruins with Stacey, the ringing of a nearby buoy almost sounded like a clock tower, chiming that it's time for tea. It was one of Stacey's first hikes in Acadia, and she was struck by the contrast of sandy beach and rocky summit. "That's very rare," said Stacey.

From the parking lot, head down the stairs to the beach and walk 0.1 mile to the farthest (easternmost) end. Cross a channel—best at low tide to keep your feet dry—to the Great Head trailhead.

Go up a series of granite steps bordered by a split-rail fence. At the top of the steps, at 0.2 mile, turn right (southeast) and follow the blue blazes up the rocky ledges. Views of Sand Beach, the Beehive, and Champlain Mountain are immediately visible.

At the next trail junction, at about 0.3 mile, bear right (south) to head toward the tip of the peninsula, with views of Old Soaker, a nearby outcropping that appears rectangular at low tide, and of Otter Cliff and the Cranberry Isles in the distance.

At 0.6 mile the trail rounds the peninsula. At 0.9 mile it reaches the summit of Great Head, where there are views of Frenchman Bay and Egg Rock.

At about 1.2 miles, along a level section of the trail, you reach a junction in a birch grove. Turn left (southwest) and ascend gradually up Great Head ridge, with views of Champlain Mountain, the Beehive, and Gorham Mountain. (If you go straight (northwest) at this junction to a parking lot near Schooner Head Road and then circle back, you can add another 0.8 mile to the loop.)

At the last junction, at 1.4 miles, bear right (northwest) to return to the trailhead and Sand Beach. Head back to the parking lot for a loop hike of 1.7 miles.

Miles and Directions

0.0   Begin at the edge of the parking lot, head down the stairs, and walk east along Sand Beach.

0.1   Cross a small channel at the east end of the beach to reach the Great Head trailhead.

0.2   Bear right (southeast) at the top of the stairs.

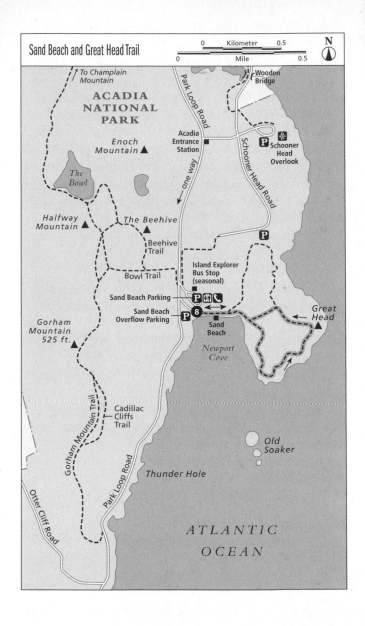

Sand Beach and Great Head Trail

0 Kilometer 0.5
0 Mile 0.5

N

To Champlain Mountain

ACADIA NATIONAL PARK

Enoch Mountain ▲

The Bowl

Halfway Mountain ▲

The Beehive ▲

Beehive Trail

Bowl Trail

Gorham Mountain 525 ft. ▲

Gorham Mountain Trail

Cadillac Cliffs Trail

Park Loop Road

Otter Cliff Road

one way

Park Loop Road

Acadia Entrance Station

Schooner Head Road

Schooner Head Overlook

Island Explorer Bus Stop (seasonal)

Sand Beach Parking

Sand Beach Overflow Parking

8

Sand Beach

Newport Cove

Great Head ▲

Wooden Bridge

Old Soaker

Thunder Hole

ATLANTIC OCEAN

0.3 At the junction with the spur trail inland, go right (south) along the shore.

0.4 Reach the south end of the Great Head peninsula and follow the trail as it curves northeast along the shore.

0.9 Arrive on the Great Head summit, where the remnants of a stone teahouse can be found.

1.2 At the junction in the birch grove with the spur trail to Great Head ridge, bear left (southwest).

1.4 Bear right (northwest) at the junction.

1.6 Arrive back at the Great Head trailhead.

1.7 Walk west along the beach back to the parking lot, completing the loop.

$\bigcirc$ Ocean Path

This easy hike takes you along Acadia's distinct pink-granite coastline, bringing you to Thunder Hole, where you may hear a reverberating boom as the surf crashes against a rocky chasm; Otter Cliff, where you may see rock climbers on the 60-foot precipice; and Otter Point, where you may catch a colorful sunset.

Distance: 4.6 miles out and back

Approximate hiking time: 2 to 2.5 hours

Difficulty: Easy

Trail surface: Graded gravel path, forest floor

Best season: Spring through fall, particularly early morning or late afternoon in the summer to avoid the crowds

Other trail users: Motorists stopping along the Park Loop Road to view Thunder Hole or Otter Point, rock climbers accessing Otter Cliff

Canine compatibility: Leashed dogs permitted

Nat Geo Trails Illustrated Topographic Map: Acadia National Park

Special considerations: Seasonal restrooms available at Sand Beach parking lot; restrooms at Thunder Hole (seasonal) and Fabbri (year-round) parking areas. A short part of Ocean Path that includes a viewing platform is accessible for visitors with wheelchairs or baby strollers, across from the first parking lot on the right, 0.3 mile south of Sand Beach.

Finding the trailhead: From the park's visitor center, drive south on the Park Loop Road for about 3 miles and turn left (east) at the sign for Sand Beach. Follow the one-way Park Loop Road for about 5.5 miles, past the park entrance station, to the beach parking lot on the left (east) side of the road. The trailhead is on the right (east) just before the stairs to the beach. The Island Explorer's Loop Road and Sand Beach lines stop at the beach parking lot. **GPS:** N44 19.45' / W68 11.01'

The Hike

The sounds of the ocean and the views of rocky cliffs and pink-granite shoreline are never far from Ocean Path. At Thunder Hole, halfway along the path, when the conditions are just right, the surf crashes through rocky chasms with a thunderous roar. And at Otter Point, at trail's end, the sound of a buoy ringing fills the air. Rock climbers can be seen scaling Otter Cliff, one of the premier rock climbing areas in the eastern United States, while picnickers, birders, and sun worshippers can be found enjoying themselves on the flat pink-granite slabs that dot the shore here.

First used as a buckboard road in the 1870s, Ocean Path and Ocean Drive were incorporated into John D. Rockefeller Jr.'s vision of scenic roads, bringing visitors to many of Mount Desert Island's unique features. He began motor-road construction in the park in 1927 and hired landscape architect Frederick Law Olmsted Jr. to lay out many of the routes, including the Otter Cliff section of Ocean Drive. Ocean Path, first described in 1874, was substantially reconstructed by the Civilian Conservation Corps during the 1930s' Great Depression, with funding assistance from Rockefeller.

Because of its ease and accessibility, Ocean Path can be crowded during the height of the tourist season. The best time to walk it is either very early or very late on a summer's day, or in the spring or fall. If you explore the shore along Ocean Path, park officials ask that you please stay on designated routes to and from the path.

Ocean Path, often worn from heavy use and storms, was substantially rehabilitated in 2015 and 2016. The work included about 0.5 mile of resurfacing, including 550 feet of paving with a porous compound that binds to gravel and is designed to prevent damage from rain runoff; forty-three new or redone steps; an access trail for the physically disabled from a small parking lot on the right 0.3 mile south of Sand Beach and across from a rocky island known as Old Soaker; and a new viewing platform just north of the Old Soaker lot.

The Ocean Path trailhead is on the right just before the stairs to Sand Beach. Follow the gravel path past the changing rooms and restrooms, up a series of stairs, and then left (south) away from a secondary parking area. The easy trail takes you southwest along the shore, paralleling the Ocean Drive section of the Park Loop Road.

Thunder Hole, a popular destination, is at 1.0 mile. Many visitors driving through the park on calm summer days stop here and cause a traffic jam but go away disappointed. It turns out the best time to experience the power of Thunder Hole is after a storm and as high tide approaches, when the surf crashes violently through the chasms, pushing trapped air against the rock and creating a sound like the clap of thunder.

But even when you know the best time to hear Thunder Hole, it can still take a number of times before you hit it right. On one trip to Acadia, we went with our nieces Sharon and Michelle to this spot three times, once late at night with stormy seas, but didn't hear the thundering boom as we expected.

If you, too, come to Thunder Hole during stormy conditions, be careful. Visitors have been swept out to sea here and at Schoodic Point, a reminder of how powerful nature can be along Acadia's coast. Watch out for large waves, stay a safe distance away, and don't turn your back on the ocean.

At 1.3 miles on Ocean Path, you pass a short series of stairs on the right (west), which lead across the Park Loop Road to the Gorham Mountain trailhead. Monument Cove, with its startling granite structures, is near this trailhead.

The path's only noticeable elevation gain comes as it rises through the woods toward Otter Cliff, reached at 1.8 miles. On the approach, you can see rock climbers scaling the rock face or waiting at the top of the cliffs for their turn. A staircase leads down on the left (east) to the rock climbers' registration board.

Ocean Path ends at 2.3 miles, at Otter Point, where you can watch the sun set over Acadia and find a nearby commemorative plaque dedicated to Rockefeller. A new bronze plaque, financed by contributions to replace the 1960s original, was dedicated in 2016 during a ceremony attended by about twenty Rockefeller family members, including the youngest of Rockefeller's six children, banker David Rockefeller Sr., who died in 2017 at the age of 101.

Return the way you came.

Miles and Directions

0.0 Start at the Ocean Path trailhead, on the right just before the stairs to Sand Beach. Follow the gravel path up a series of stairs and then left (south) away from a secondary parking area.

1.0 Reach Thunder Hole (a viewing platform there may be closed during stormy seas).

1.3 Pass the Gorham Mountain trailhead, which is across the Park Loop Road.

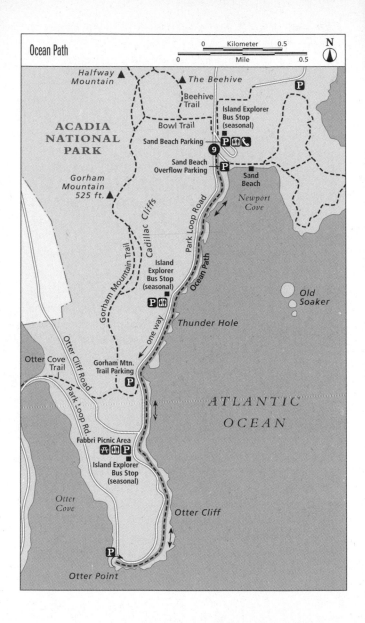

1.8 Reach Otter Cliff, where you can see rock climbers scaling the precipice.

2.3 Arrive at Otter Point, where you can watch the sun set.

4.6 Arrive back at the trailhead.

10 The Bowl Trail

This hike leads to a mountain pond called the Bowl, where you can encounter wildlife, especially if you travel early in the morning or late in the afternoon. You can connect to the Gorham Mountain and Champlain South Ridge Trails off this trail. And you can find more moderate ascents up the back side of the nearby Beehive, a nice alternative to climbing the iron ladder rungs up that peak's cliff.

Distance: 1.6 miles out and back

Approximate hiking time: 1.5 to 2 hours

Difficulty: Moderate

Trail surface: Forest floor, rock ledges

Best season: Spring through fall, particularly early morning or late afternoon in the summer to avoid the crowds

Other trail users: Hikers climbing the Beehive

Canine compatibility: Leashed dogs permitted (but not on the ladder climb up the Beehive)

Nat Geo Trails Illustrated Topographic Map: Acadia National Park

Special considerations: Seasonal restrooms and a pay phone at Sand Beach parking lot

Finding the trailhead: From the park's visitor center, drive south on the Park Loop Road for about 3 miles and turn left (east) at the sign for Sand Beach. Follow the one-way Park Loop Road for about 5.5 miles, past the park entrance station, to the beach parking lot on the left (east) side of the road. The Island Explorer's Loop Road and Sand Beach lines stop at the beach parking lot. The trailhead is diagonally (northwest) across the Park Loop Road from the beach parking lot. **GPS:** N44 19.54' / W68 11.07'

The Hike

Views of a great blue heron taking off low across the water's surface or of a turkey vulture soaring high on the thermals are among the possible rewards when you hike to the Bowl, a mountain pond at more than 400 feet in elevation.

We were lucky and got both views in the same day as we hiked along the shoreline. Another time, during a walk down from the Bowl, we heard a loud snorting in the woods. A couple of white-tailed deer darted through the trees, the snorting apparently an alarm call. Hike in the early morning or late afternoon to improve your chances of such wildlife encounters.

The Bowl Trail begins by climbing gradually through a lowland birch forest, passing a junction with the very steep Beehive Trail, featuring iron ladder rungs, at 0.2 mile.

Recent rerouting of the next portion of the Bowl Trail has eased the gradient a bit and lengthened the distance by 0.1 mile so that a spur to the Gorham Mountain Trail is now at 0.5 mile, and another spur to the Beehive, a more gradual alternative to the ladder approach, is at 0.6 mile, at the same place where the Gorham Mountain Trail comes in.

Beyond, the Bowl Trail heads up steeply through the woods, then goes downhill, arriving at the Bowl at the 0.8-mile mark. This also marks the junction with the 1.6-mile Champlain South Ridge Trail, which heads left (northwest), and another moderate spur to the Beehive, which heads right (east).

Return the way you came.

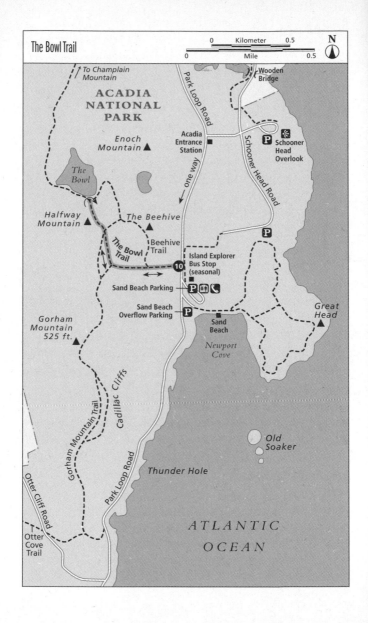

The Bowl Trail

| 0 | Kilometer | 0.5 |
| 0 | Mile | 0.5 |

N

To Champlain
Mountain

ACADIA
NATIONAL
PARK

Park Loop Road

Wooden
Bridge

Enoch
Mountain ▲

Acadia
Entrance
Station

Schooner Head Road

P Schooner
Head
Overlook

The
Bowl

Halfway
Mountain ▲

The Beehive
▲

Beehive
Trail

P

The Bowl
Trail

10 Island Explorer
Bus Stop
(seasonal)

Sand Beach Parking P

Sand Beach
Overflow Parking P

Sand
Beach

Great
Head

Gorham
Mountain
525 ft. ▲

Newport
Cove

Gorham Mountain Trail

Cadillac Cliffs

Old
Soaker

Park Loop Road

Thunder Hole

Otter Cliff Road

Otter
Cove
Trail

ATLANTIC
OCEAN

Miles and Directions

0.0 Start at the Bowl trailhead, diagonally (northwest) across the Park Loop Road from the Sand Beach parking lot.

0.2 Reach the junction with the Beehive Trail, a very steep ladder climb that heads right, up that peak's cliff.

0.5 A spur trail to the Gorham Mountain Trail heads left at this junction.

0.6 A more moderate spur trail up the Beehive heads right at this junction. The Gorham Mountain Trail heads left at this junction.

0.8 Arrive at the Bowl and the junction with the Champlain South Ridge Trail and another moderate spur trail up the Beehive.

1.6 Arrive back at the trailhead.

11 Gorham Mountain Trail

This is a classic Acadia hike to a 525-foot peak with sweeping views of Great Head, Sand Beach, Otter Cliff, Champlain Mountain, and the Beehive. The trail, among the most traveled in the park, is also one of the most historic, dating back to the early 1900s and the Great Depression. The hike includes a spur trail to Cadillac Cliffs and an ancient sea cave.

Distance: 1.8 miles out and back
Approximate hiking time: 1 to 1.5 hours
Difficulty: Moderate
Trail surface: Forest floor, rock ledges, rock steps
Best season: Spring through fall, particularly early morning or late afternoon in the summer to avoid the crowds
Other trail users: Campers at Blackwoods Campground hiking up Gorham via the Quarry and Otter Cove Trails

Canine compatibility: Leashed dogs permitted (but not recommended on the optional Cadillac Cliffs Trail, which features a couple of iron rungs)
Nat Geo Trails Illustrated Topographic Map: Acadia National Park
Special considerations: No facilities at trailhead, but nearby restrooms at Thunder Hole (seasonal) and Fabbri (year-round) parking areas

Finding the trailhead: From the park's visitor center, drive south on the Park Loop Road for about 3 miles and turn left (east) at the sign for Sand Beach. Follow the one-way Park Loop Road for about 7 miles, passing the park entrance station, Sand Beach, and Thunder Hole, to the Gorham Mountain sign and parking lot on the right (west) side of the road. The Island Explorer bus does not have a stop here, although the Sand Beach and Park Loop lines go by, and you may be able to ask the bus driver to let you off if it is safe to do so. **GPS:** N44 19.00' / W68 11.28'

The Hike

Charlie Jacobi, a retired ranger at Acadia National Park, estimates that he's hiked the Gorham Mountain Trail maybe 300 times over the years, mostly as part of the job. But he says it never gets old.

"Every day is different," said Jacobi during a recent hike on a sunny afternoon to the peak of Gorham, noted for some of the most rewarding views in Acadia.

The trail is among the most popular in the park, and it's easy to see why.

"This whole ridge—Gorham, Champlain, and the Beehive—is close to the ocean," says Jacobi, who retired in 2017 after working thirty-three years at the park. "You're right on top of it—almost. That's what makes it attractive."

The trail, marked by historic-style cairns that Jacobi helped reintroduce to the park, follows the great ridge that runs all the way to Champlain Mountain and is the closest to the ocean of all of Acadia's mountain ridges.

An additional bonus, if you choose to take it, is the 0.5-mile spur trail to the once-submerged Cadillac Cliffs and an ancient sea cave, which illustrates the powerful geologic forces that helped shape Mount Desert Island.

From the parking lot, bypass the Otter Cove Trail that connects to Blackwoods Campground and comes in on the left (southwest) near the trailhead. Bear right on the Gorham Mountain Trail to climb gradually through an evergreen forest and up open ledges, heading north. Though the trail is often shaded by conifers in this section, the sounds of the ocean surf signal that the shore is nearby.

At 0.2 mile the Cadillac Cliffs Trail leads right (northeast), paralleling and then rejoining the Gorham Mountain Trail at 0.5 mile. (If you want to add the Cadillac Cliffs spur, it is best to do it on the ascent rather than the descent, because of the iron rungs and steep rock face along the way.) Don't miss a bronze memorial at this intersection honoring Waldron Bates, chair of the Roads and Paths Committee of the Bar Harbor Village Improvement Association from 1900 to 1909, who developed the century-old style of cairn now used to mark many Acadia trails.

Stay on the Gorham Mountain Trail and ascend moderately; a near-barren island called Old Soaker comes into sight through the trees.

All along this portion of the route you will enjoy views south to Otter Cliff, northeast to Great Head and Sand Beach, and north to the Beehive and Champlain Mountain. Frenchman Bay and Egg Rock can be seen in the distance to the east.

We stop when we spot a Bates-style cairn in need of repair.

In 2002, Jacobi and Gary Stellpflug, foreman of the Acadia trails crew, revived the use of the Bates-style cairns, which consist of two to four base stones, with a lintel laid across them, that is capped by a pointer stone.

The Gorham Mountain Trail is home to fifty-one such cairns and was part of a research study that Jacobi led to test the effectiveness of signs in discouraging people from stacking stone, dismantling, or otherwise damaging the cairns. As one sign near a cairn cautioned, adding or removing rocks misleads hikers, causes erosion or kills plants and degrades the mountain landscape.

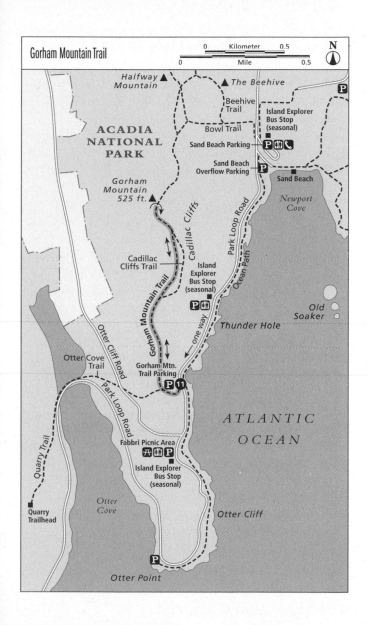

Gorham Mountain Trail

0   Kilometer   0.5

0   Mile   0.5

N

Halfway Mountain   ▲ The Beehive

P

Beehive Trail

Island Explorer Bus Stop (seasonal)

ACADIA NATIONAL PARK

Bowl Trail

Sand Beach Parking   P 🚻 📞

Sand Beach Overflow Parking   P

Gorham Mountain 525 ft. ▲

Sand Beach

Newport Cove

Cadillac Cliffs

Cadillac Cliffs Trail

Island Explorer Bus Stop (seasonal)

P 🚻

Park Loop Road

Ocean Path

one way

Thunder Hole

Old Soaker

Gorham Mountain Trail

Otter Cliff Road

Otter Cove Trail

Gorham Mtn. Trail Parking

P 11

ATLANTIC OCEAN

Park Loop Road

Quarry Trail

Fabbri Picnic Area   🏕 🚻 P

Island Explorer Bus Stop (seasonal)

Otter Cove

Otter Cliff

Quarry Trailhead

P

Otter Point

We reach the peak of Gorham Mountain at 0.9 mile. At the 525-foot summit, looking northeast, Jacobi points out the backside of the Beehive.

To the north, a small hill called Halfway Mountain is situated below Champlain Mountain and Huguenot Head, and to the west are Dorr and Cadillac Mountains.

On the mainland in the distance is Schoodic Mountain with its radio tower, and then the Schoodic Peninsula to the east. And the Cranberry Islands, including Baker Island and its 1855 light tower, are to the south.

Return the way you came.

On the trek down, listen for the sounds of a bell buoy located near an ocean ledge. On a day when the sky is blue and the sun bright, the ocean can appear almost tropical.

"Oh my God," said Jacobi. "This is spectacular."

No matter how many times you hike the Gorham Mountain Trail, it always seems rewarding.

Miles and Directions

0.0 Start at the Gorham Mountain trailhead, which leaves from a parking lot on the right (west) side of the one-way Park Loop Road. Coming in on the left just after the trailhead is the Otter Cove Trail that links to Blackwoods Campground. Bear right at the junction to continue on the Gorham Mountain Trail.

0.2 Reach the junction with the southern end of the Cadillac Cliffs Trail. Stay straight to continue on Gorham Mountain Trail.

0.5 Pass the junction with the northern end of the Cadillac Cliffs Trail, which comes in from the right (east).

0.9 Arrive on the Gorham Mountain summit.

1.8 Arrive back at the trailhead.

12 Quarry and Otter Cove Trails

This two-section hike is for people staying at the Blackwoods Campground or for hikers eager to explore two of the newest trails in the park. The trails, inaugurated on June 7, 2014, are excellent for campers seeking either a hike to Gorham Mountain, Sand Beach, or Thunder Hole or just a short walk to Otter Cove. An endowment from the Friends of Acadia helped finance construction of the trails. Volunteers from the Friends and the Acadia Youth Conservation Corps helped the Park Service construct the trails.

Distance: 1.8 miles out and back

Approximate hiking time: 1 to 1.5 hours

Difficulty: Easy

Trail surface: Graded gravel path, forest floor, grassy strip along the Park Loop Road

Best season: Spring through fall, particularly early morning or late afternoon in the summer to avoid the crowds

Other trail users: Motorists or bicyclists exploring Otter Cove along the Park Loop Road, other hikers coming from the Gorham Mountain Trail

Canine compatibility: Leashed dogs permitted

Nat Geo Trails Illustrated Topographic Map: Acadia National Park

Special considerations: Full facilities available seasonally at Blackwoods Campground

Finding the trailhead: For campers and guests at the Blackwoods Campground, walk to the entrance station and across the road to the trailhead, northeast of the entrance station. For day hikers in season, take the Island Explorer Sand Beach line to Blackwoods Campground. **GPS:** N44 18.37' / W68 12.13'

The Hike

Amid the sounds of buoy bells from the nearby Atlantic Ocean, the Quarry Trail starts along fresh, packed gravel just outside the entrance station of the Blackwoods Campground.

Named for a quarry that used to operate in the area, the trail follows an overhead electric power line and then bears right along a graded path. Soon the cove comes into view through pine trees on the right; intermittent stone steps and wooden cribbing, or interlocked logs, help guide a some- times steep descent to the cove.

The hike reaches a triple-arch, stone bridge along a causeway of the one-way Park Loop Road over the cove, at 0.4 mile. The trail offers great views north over intertidal mudflats toward Dorr and Cadillac Mountains and south to Otter Cove, as it ends at the Park Loop Road.

Turn left (northeast) to pick up the Otter Cove Trail as it starts on a grassy route along the loop road and eventually takes you through a large grove of ash trees. The trail quickly ascends to a wooden footbridge and then a second, tiny foot- bridge. It crosses over Otter Cliff Road at 0.7 mile, goes over a third wooden bridge, and ends at the Gorham Mountain Trail at 0.9 mile.

Return the way you came. If you want to explore further, there are a couple of options: Turn left (northwest) to ascend less than a mile to 525-foot Gorham. Or bear right (east) toward the Gorham Mountain parking lot, cross the Park Loop Road, and take a left (north) along Ocean Path, reach- ing Thunder Hole in 0.3 mile and Sand Beach in 1.3 miles.

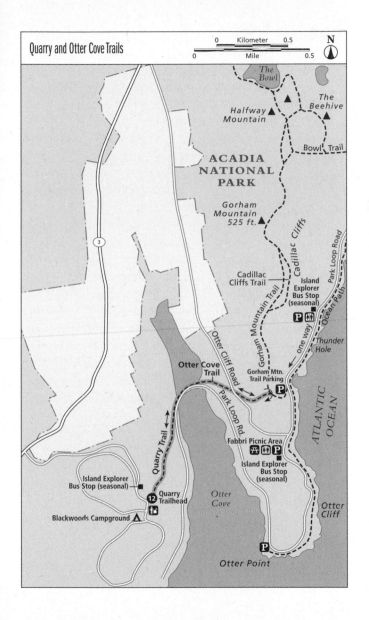

Quarry and Otter Cove Trails

0   Kilometer   0.5

0   Mile   0.5

N

The Bowl

Halfway Mountain

The Beehive

ACADIA NATIONAL PARK

Bowl Trail

Gorham Mountain 525 ft.

Cadillac Cliffs

Park Loop Road

Cadillac Cliffs Trail

Island Explorer Bus Stop (seasonal)

Ocean Path

Gorham Mountain Trail

one way

Thunder Hole

Otter Cove Trail

Gorham Mtn. Trail Parking

Otter Cliff Road

ATLANTIC OCEAN

Park Loop Rd

Fabbri Picnic Area

Island Explorer Bus Stop (seasonal)

Quarry Trail

Island Explorer Bus Stop (seasonal)

12 Quarry Trailhead

Blackwoods Campground

Otter Cove

Otter Cliff

Otter Point

Miles and Directions

0.0   Start at the Quarry trailhead, to the left (east) of the Black-woods Campground entrance station.

0.4   Reach the Park Loop Road at the Otter Cove causeway. Turn left (northeast) to pick up Otter Cove Trail as it starts on a grassy strip along the loop road.

0.7   Cross Otter Cliff Road.

0.9   Reach the junction with Gorham Mountain Trail.

1.8   Arrive back at the trailhead.

13 Jordan Pond Path (Jordan Pond Shore Trail)

This hike offers expansive views of Jordan Pond, the Bubbles, and Jordan Cliffs, as well as a chance to glimpse a colorful merganser duck or busy beaver, or watch kayakers plying the waters. The graded gravel path on the east side of the pond is particularly easy, and an amazing 4,000 feet of log bridges on the west side helps smooth the way over what would otherwise be a potentially wet, rocky, and root-filled trail.

Distance: 3.3-mile loop
Approximate hiking time: 1.5 to 2 hours
Difficulty: Easy
Trail surface: Graded gravel path, rock slabs, forest floor, log bridges, log boardwalk
Best season: Spring through fall, particularly early morning or late afternoon in the summer to avoid the crowds
Other trail users: Motorists using the Jordan Pond boat ramp road that crosses the trail to unload their canoes or kayaks, people walking their bikes to the nearby Jordan Pond House

Canine compatibility: Leashed dogs permitted on the trail, but not in Jordan Pond
Nat Geo Trails Illustrated Topographic Map: Acadia National Park
Special considerations: Certain sections of the graded gravel path on the east, west, and south sides of pond are accessible to wheelchairs and baby strollers. There is a chemical toilet at the trailhead; full facilities are available seasonally at nearby Jordan Pond House.

Finding the trailhead: From the park's visitor center, head south on the Park Loop Road for about 7.6 miles and turn right (north) into the Jordan Pond north lot. Park in the lot on the right. Follow the boat ramp road down to the shore of the pond. The trailhead is on the right (east) and leads around the pond. The Island Explorer's Loop Road and Jordan Pond lines stop at the nearby Jordan Pond House. **GPS:** N44 19.22' / W68 15.13'

The Hike

A vigorous walk around Jordan Pond, capped by afternoon tea and popovers on the lawn of the Jordan Pond House—it's one of those special Acadia experiences.

The trail starts from the end of the boat ramp road at the Jordan Pond north parking lot and immediately offers a spectacular view of the rounded mountains known as the Bubbles, which lie north across the pond. Bear right (east), circling the pond counterclockwise.

The first half of the trail is along the easy eastern shore with its graded gravel path, but be prepared for the western shore's rock slabs and long series of log bridges known as a bogwalk. The rocks and log bridges can be slippery when wet. Wear proper footwear.

At 0.2 mile you reach the first of several trails that diverge from the Jordan Pond Path. Bear left, paralleling the shore at each of the junctions. The trail rounds a bend at the south end of the pond, across a rock path that was originally built in the early 1900s, providing pond and wetlands views.

At 0.3 mile pass the junction with the Bubble & Jordan Ponds Path (Pond Trail), which leads to trails up Pemetic Mountain. Stay on Jordan Pond Path along the eastern shore of the pond.

The trail now begins heading north. You soon start seeing Jordan Cliffs to the west across the pond. There are plenty of boulders along the shore to sit on and admire the crystal-clear waters and the tremendous views. Jordan Pond serves as a public water supply, so no swimming is allowed.

After passing over a series of wood bridges, you soon come up under the towering pinkish granite of South Bubble near the north side of the pond.

At 1.1 miles you reach Jordan Pond Carry and the Bubbles Trail (South Bubble Trail), which veer to the right (north) and lead, respectively, to Eagle Lake and South Bubble.

At 1.6 miles pass the junction with Bubbles Divide, a trail that heads right (northeast) up the gap between North and South Bubbles and allows access to the precariously perched Bubble Rock, which is visible from the Park Loop Road. You are now at the northernmost end of the pond and can get good views of the Jordan Pond House to the south and the Bubbles to the east. Cross a series of intricate wood bridges—one rustic-style span has an archway in the middle.

At 1.7 miles pass the junction with the Deer Brook Trail, which leads up toward Penobscot Mountain and provides access to the Jordan Cliffs Trail and the beautiful double-arch Deer Brook Bridge, built in 1925 as part of the carriage road system. The Deer Brook Trail was the setting for a scene in the Stephen King movie *Pet Sematary*.

Now begins the trail's traverse of the rougher western shore of the pond, with its rock slabs and long series of log bridges. After a bit of hide-and-seek with the shore and a stretch of rock hopping, you reach the log bridges that take you over fragile wetlands.

In addition to the dramatic views of the Bubbles, you may also catch a glimpse of a common merganser, as we did. It is hard to miss a merganser, especially a female, with its rust-colored, crested head and orange bill. Evidence of

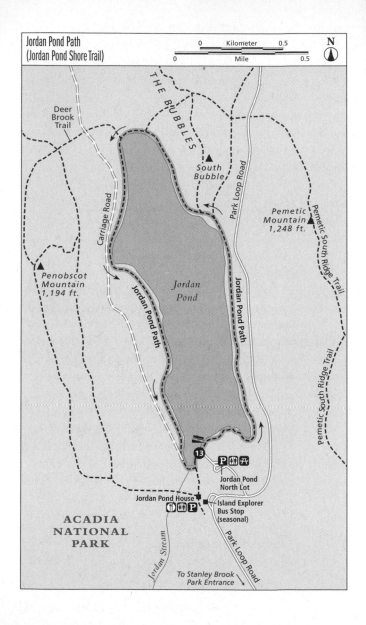

Jordan Pond Path
(Jordan Pond Shore Trail)

0   Kilometer   0.5

0   Mile   0.5

N

THE BUBBLES

Deer Brook Trail

South Bubble

Carriage Road

Pemetic Mountain 1,248 ft.

Pemetic South Ridge Trail

Penobscot Mountain 1,194 ft.

Jordan Pond Path

Jordan Pond

Jordan Pond Path

Pemetic South Ridge Trail

13

P 🚻 ⛺

Jordan Pond North Lot

Jordan Pond House
🚻 P

Island Explorer Bus Stop (seasonal)

ACADIA NATIONAL PARK

Jordan Stream

Park Loop Road

To Stanley Brook Park Entrance

beaver activity dots the shore of Jordan Pond, and you may also see a beaver chowing down, as we have.

At 3.2 miles turn left onto the carriage road and cross a carriage road bridge. Then turn left again to follow the trail as it circles back to the Jordan Pond north lot at 3.3 miles. Just before you get back to the lot, you can turn right (south) and head up the hill to the Jordan Pond House for an Acadia tradition of afternoon tea and popovers, with a grand view of the pond and the Bubbles as nature's backdrop.

Miles and Directions

0.0 Start at the Jordan Pond Path trailhead. At the end of the boat ramp road, turn right along the graded gravel path.

0.2 Bear left at a junction and continue straight along the eastern shore of the pond.

0.3 Reach the junction with the Bubbles and Jordan Pond Path (Pond Trail) and continue straight along the eastern shore of the pond.

1.1 Reach the junction with Jordan Pond Carry and the Bubbles Trail (South Bubble Trail) and continue straight along the eastern shore of the pond.

1.6 Reach the junction with Bubbles Divide, which goes northeast through the gap between North and South Bubbles. Continue along the shore as the path rounds the north side of the pond.

1.7 Reach the junction with the Deer Brook Trail, which leads up Penobscot Mountain. Continue along the shore of the pond with the path now following the west side.

3.2 Turn left onto the carriage road and cross a carriage road bridge, then turn left again to follow the path as it circles back to the Jordan Pond north lot.

3.3 Arrive back at the trailhead, completing the loop.

14 Jordan Stream Path

It's a crisp woods walk from the Jordan Pond House along the meandering Jordan Stream to the main highlight of this trail: a carriage road bridge faced with cobblestones rather than the granite that surfaces other bridges in the carriage road system. Once badly eroded, this path benefits from a recent rehabilitation that includes patio-style stone steps along the shore, rebuilt wooden bridges, and new bogwalk.

Distance: 1.2 miles out and back

Approximate hiking time: 30 minutes to 1 hour

Difficulty: Easy to moderate

Trail surface: Wooden bridges, stone steps, forest floor

Best season: Spring through fall

Other trail users: Passengers getting off a horse-drawn carriage to see Cobblestone Bridge

Canine compatibility: Leashed dogs permitted

Nat Geo Trails Illustrated Topographic Map: Acadia National Park

Special considerations: Full seasonal facilities at the Jordan Pond House

Finding the trailhead: From the park's visitor center, drive south on the Park Loop Road for about 7.6 miles and turn right (north) into the Jordan Pond north lot. Park in the lot on the left (south) and follow signs to the Jordan Pond House. Walk behind and to the right (west) of the Jordan Pond House and follow a path marked "To Asticou & Jordan Pond Path, Spring Trail, Penobscot & Sargent Mtn Trails" down to a carriage road; the trailhead is across the carriage road on the left. The Island Explorer's Loop Road and Jordan Pond lines stop at the Jordan Pond House. **GPS:** N44 19.13' / W68 15.19'

The Hike

Jordan Stream Path is among the shortest and easiest hikes in Acadia National Park, but it ends at one of the park's most unusual and historic landmarks: Cobblestone Bridge.

Previously worn and overrun with roots, the path benefited from extensive rehabilitation in 2015 overseen by Christian Barter, a park trail crew supervisor who is also the park's poet laureate. The work included rebuilding four wooden bridges, totaling 59 feet; rerouting 300 feet of the path higher and farther from the stream; and adding about 400 feet of bogwalk, or wide double planks close to the ground; a patio-style stone walkway next to the stream; and new signs and drainage systems.

Jordan Stream, a habitat for sea-run brook trout, seems like something out of a Robert Frost poem, with small waterfalls, pools, and rushing water in season. The stream starts at the south end of Jordan Pond and goes all the way to Little Long Pond near Seal Harbor.

The path was laid out more than a century ago by the Seal Harbor Village Improvement Association as a scenic connector between the village and Jordan Pond. It starts near the busy Jordan Pond House, but it is often overlooked by hikers who opt for more prominent hikes in the area.

Jim Linnane, a volunteer crew leader with the Friends of Acadia, whose volunteers helped in the path rehabilitation, noted that thick spruce forests—untouched by the great fire of 1947—help keep the path often private and quiet.

"Hiking the Jordan Stream trail, I often think about how special it is, especially because it is so close to the mass of humanity that descends on the Jordan Pond area on a nice day," Linnane said. "Surprisingly, even after a very dry summer, the Jordan Stream still has some running water. The gurgle and trickle of the stream is a welcome and wonderful interruption to the silence of the deep woods."

The path, probably once part of a Native American canoe carry trail linking Jordan Pond to the ocean, is within park boundaries for about a half mile, but just outside the park, it reaches the famed Cobblestone Bridge, the only span in the carriage road system faced with naturally rounded cobblestones. The other bridges are surfaced with granite.

The 150-foot-long, 21-foot-high bridge was built in 1917 and was the first major structure constructed as part of the carriage road system on Mount Desert Island, according to *Acadia's Carriage Roads*, by Robert A. Thayer.

Sixteen of the seventeen bridges were paid for by John D. Rockefeller Jr., the only son of the founder of a giant oil company; the last was financed by the park in 1941. Rockefeller came up with the idea for the carriage roads and oversaw details of construction starting in 1913, with 45 miles currently within the park boundaries.

While the hike's destination, the Cobblestone Bridge, is much photographed now, it may not always have been so well loved.

According to *Rockefeller Carriage Roads*, a Historic American Engineering Record report that stems from research administered by the National Park Service from 1994 to 1995, George B. Dorr, Acadia's first park superintendent, criticized the bridge's construction in a 1924 letter to Park Service assistant director Arno B. Cammerer, writing that "all have agreed in regretting it from the artistic standpoint," but it would soon be "little noticeable" because vegetation was closing around it.

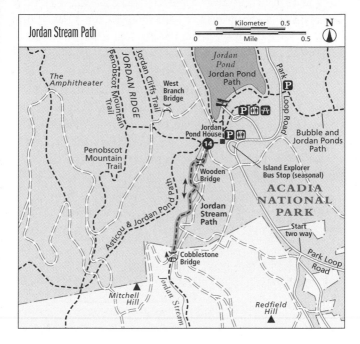

The report says Rockefeller had planned for a granite-faced bridge, but his engineer, Charles Simpson, instead urged the use of native cobbles, or rounded stones from the streambed.

Jordan Stream Path itself is easy to reach, with the trailhead located at the carriage road behind the Jordan Pond House.

Follow the narrow path through the woods, paralleling the stream as it tumbles south toward the ocean. Part of the trail features more than thirty neatly laid stepping-stones, making it seem like a garden path at times.

When you reach a junction with a carriage road at 0.2 mile, bear right (west) across a wooden bridge. Pick up the trail at the end of the bridge, heading left (south) down the other side of the stream.

The trail descends, and a series of wooden footbridges take you across stream tributaries.

At 0.6 mile the trail brings you to the base of the Cobblestone Bridge. The trail continues toward Seal Harbor across private land, making the bridge a natural turnaround point.

Return the way you came.

Miles and Directions

0.0 Start at the Jordan Stream Path trailhead, behind and to the right (west) of the Jordan Pond House.

0.2 Reach a junction with a carriage road. Cross a wooden bridge to the right (west) and continue south down the trail along the western bank of Jordan Stream.

0.6 Reach Cobblestone Bridge.

1.2 Arrive back at the trailhead.

15 Bubbles Divide (Bubble Rock Trail)

A moderate hike with some steep stretches brings you to 360-degree views from South Bubble and an up-close perspective of Bubble Rock, a precariously perched glacial erratic visible from the Park Loop Road that generations of hikers have playfully attempted to "push." From South Bubble, Jordan Pond and the Atlantic Ocean are to the south, Pemetic Mountain to the east, North Bubble to the north, and Sargent and Penobscot Mountains to the west.

Distance: 1.0 mile out and back
Approximate hiking time: 1 hour
Difficulty: Moderate to more challenging
Trail surface: Forest floor, rock ledges, log steps
Best season: Spring through fall, particularly early morning or late afternoon in summer to avoid the crowds
Other trail users: Hikers accessing North Bubble, Eagle Lake, or Jordan Pond

Canine compatibility: Leashed dogs permitted
Nat Geo Trails Illustrated Topographic Map: Acadia National Park
Special considerations: No facilities at trailhead; chemical toilet at Jordan Pond north lot and full seasonal facilities at Jordan Pond House, a short drive away

Finding the trailhead: From the park's visitor center, drive south on the Park Loop Road for about 6 miles, past the Cadillac Mountain entrance and the Bubble Pond parking lot, to the Bubble Rock parking lot on the right (west) side of the road. The trailhead departs from the Bubble Rock parking lot. There's a new Island Explorer stop at the Bubble Rock parking lot on the Jordan Pond and Loop Road lines, but you may still need to ask the bus driver to let you off. **GPS:** N44 20.27' / W68 15.00'

The Hike

By going up into the gap between South and North Bubbles, this historic trail, dating back to the late 1800s, provides the shortest ascent to either of the rounded mountains that overlook Jordan Pond. The trip also goes to Bubble Rock, a glacially deposited boulder known as an erratic, which sits atop South Bubble, and which generations of hikers have been photographed vainly trying to "push."

Heading west from the Bubble Rock parking lot, the trail crosses Jordan Pond Carry at 0.1 mile. At the junction with the northern section of the Bubbles Trail (North Bubble Trail) at 0.2 mile, stay straight. At the junction with the southern section of the Bubbles Trail (South Bubble Trail) at 0.3 mile, turn left (south) to South Bubble and Bubble Rock.

Follow the blue blazes and cairns along the trail and reach the 768-foot South Bubble summit at 0.5 mile. A sign points left (east) to nearby Bubble Rock, dumped here by glaciers countless years ago from a spot more than 20 miles to the northeast, according to the National Park Service.

Close inspection of the 100-ton rock reveals large black and white crystals that are unlike the native pink granite of Acadia, an indication that Bubble Rock came from afar. Generations ago, it was thought that floods of biblical proportions moved giant boulders around. But it was clues like Bubble Rock that led nineteenth-century scientist Louis Agassiz to theorize that massive glaciers once covered the earth.

Return the way you came. Hardy hikers can make a 1.4-mile loop by heading steeply down the Bubbles Trail

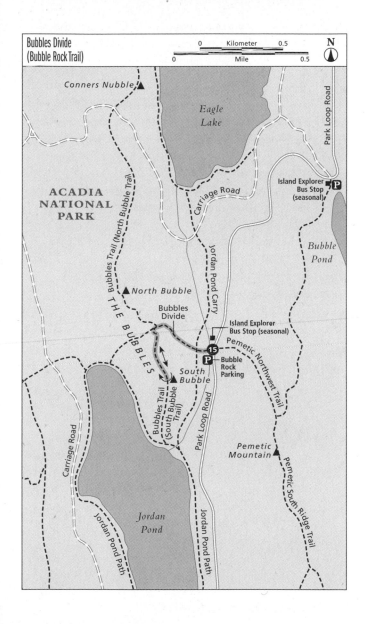

Bubbles Divide
(Bubble Rock Trail)

0   Kilometer   0.5
0   Mile   0.5

N

Conners Nubble

Eagle Lake

Park Loop Road

Carriage Road

Island Explorer Bus Stop (seasonal)

ACADIA NATIONAL PARK

Bubble Pond

THE BUBBLES

North Bubble

Jordan Pond Carry

Bubbles Divide

Island Explorer Bus Stop (seasonal)

The Bubbles Trail (North Bubble Trail)

15

Bubble Rock Parking

Pemetic Northwest Trail

South Bubble

Bubbles Trail (South Bubble Trail)

Park Loop Road

Pemetic Mountain

Carriage Road

Jordan Pond Path

Pemetic South Ridge Trail

Jordan Pond

Jordan Pond Path

(South Bubble Trail) to the shores of Jordan Pond and turning sharply left (northeast) onto Jordan Pond Carry and then
right (east) onto Bubbles Divide back to the parking lot.

Miles and Directions

0.0 Start at the Bubbles Divide trailhead, leaving from the Bubble Rock parking lot on the right (west) side of the Park Loop
Road.

0.1 Cross the junction with Jordan Pond Carry.

0.2 Reach the junction with the northern section of the Bubbles
Trail (North Bubble Trail), which comes in from the right
(north). Stay straight.

0.3 Turn left (south) onto the southern section of the Bubbles
Trail (South Bubble Trail).

0.5 Reach the South Bubble summit and Bubble Rock.

1.0 Arrive back at the trailhead.

Mount Desert Island
West of Somes Sound

This is the quieter side of the island. The major "best easy" Acadia National Park trails on the west side of Mount Desert Island go up or around such landmarks as Acadia and Flying Mountains, Beech Mountain, Beech Cliff, and Ship Harbor.

The most popular routes in the western mountains of the park are the Acadia Mountain and Flying Mountain Trails, which offer close-up views of Somes Sound, the only fjord-like estuary on the East Coast of the United States; the trail up Beech Mountain to its fire tower; and the route to Beech Cliff, with its views down to Echo Lake.

The popular and easy trails to Ship Harbor, Wonderland, and Bass Harbor Head Light are near Bass Harbor. They go along the rocky pink-granite shore that makes Acadia stand out.

16 Acadia Mountain Trail

The hike to 681-foot Acadia Mountain is along one of the older trails in the park and leads to a beautiful outlook of Somes Sound, the only fjord-like feature on the Atlantic coast of the United States, and of nearby mountains such as Norumbega and Beech. Another good option is a short side trip to Man o' War Brook, named for the French and British warships in the 1700s that came to get drinkable water where the brook cascades into Somes Sound.

Distance: 2.8-mile lollipop
Approximate hiking time: 1.5 to 2 hours
Difficulty: More challenging
Trail surface: Forest floor, rock ledges
Best season: Spring through fall, particularly early morning or late afternoon in the summer to avoid the crowds
Other trail users: Horseback riders are allowed on the Man o' War Brook Trail section of the hike

Canine compatibility: Leashed dogs permitted, but not recommended because of some steep sections
Nat Geo Trails Illustrated Topographic Map: Acadia National Park
Special considerations: Chemical toilet at parking lot across from the trailhead

Finding the trailhead: From Somesville head south on ME 102 for about 3 miles, past Ikes Point, to the Acadia Mountain parking lot on the right (west) side of ME 102. The trailhead is on the left (east) side of the road; be careful crossing the high-speed road. A new Island Explorer bus stop on the Southwest Harbor line is on the east side of ME 102, diagonally across from the Acadia Mountain parking lot. **GPS:** N44 19.18' / W68 19.57'

The Hike

A popular trek on the west side of Somes Sound because of its great views, the Acadia Mountain Trail also offers a couple of unusual features: It goes along the sole mountain ridge on Mount Desert Island that runs east to west instead of north to south, and it takes you to a waterfall that tumbles into Somes Sound.

Benjamin F. DeCosta, who explored more remote parts of the island for his *Rambles in Mount Desert*, described this trail in 1871, around the time the island first became quite popular with hikers, according to *Pathmakers*, by the National Park Service's Olmsted Center for Landscape Preservation. Formerly called Robinson Mountain, Acadia is among many peaks in the park that were renamed under George B. Dorr's leadership as first park superintendent in the early 1900s, according to *Pathmakers*.

Severe erosion once hampered hikers on this trail, but in 2016 the trails crew and the Friends of Acadia–supported Youth Conservation Corps completed a facelift on a section that includes 135 new steps, repairs to other steps, and more than 200 square feet of retaining wall.

The trail is easy at the start. From the trailhead across from the parking lot, turn immediately left (north) onto a new spur trail that parallels ME 102 and takes you to the Island Explorer bus stop at 0.1 mile. At the bus stop head east into the woods and onto the gravel Man o' War Brook Trail, an old fire road. At 0.2 mile turn left (northeast) to pick up the Acadia Mountain Trail, across from the junction with St. Sauveur Trail.

The trail continues its steady rise through cedar and pine, then heads up a rocky section with switchbacks. Good views of the sound are right ahead, and you may hear the sounds of boats.

To the west, Echo Lake comes into view behind you. The trail levels off a bit, and soon a couple of historic Bates-style cairns tip you off to the peak. Here, from a rock promontory you get expansive views of Somes Sound to the north, and the Gulf of Maine, Sutton Island, and the rest of the Cranberry Isles to the south.

Somes Sound had long been considered the East Coast's only fjord, a long, narrow, glacially carved ocean inlet, and is still listed as such on some of the park information. But in 1998 the Maine Geological Survey noted that it may be more properly described as a *fjard*, smaller than and not as limited in water circulation as a true fjord.

Atop Acadia you may find turkey vultures soaring overhead, unmistakable with their massive size and small red heads, or see and hear a peregrine falcon, as we have. Turn around here for a shorter out-and-back hike of 1.6 miles, or continue on to complete the 2.8-mile lollipop.

If you choose to go on ahead, a tricky turn on the trail directs you over jagged rock to a second peak of sorts at 1.1 miles. This second broad, open summit provides a splendid view—perhaps one of the best on the island. From here Beech Mountain with its fire tower is to the west; Valley Cove, Flying Mountain, and the Gulf of Maine are to the south; and Somes Sound and Norumbega Mountain are to the east.

The trail descends steeply from this second peak, providing close-up views of the sound on the way down. At times it's handy to hold on to trees and rocks while headed down the rock face and crevices.

At 1.7 miles you reach a junction with a spur trail to Man o'War Brook Trail and a side trail to Man o'War Brook. Turn left (east) onto the side trail, and at 1.8 miles follow stone steps to a nice spot at the base of a waterfall. When we were here in early June, the waterfall splashed along 20 to 30 feet of rock face and spilled into the sound. And during a visit in September, we saw a bald eagle fly by within 20 feet.

Return to the junction with the spur to the Man o'War Brook Trail, an old fire road, and go straight (west) on the spur trail to a major trail intersection with signs pointing to the old fire road and other points of interest. Bear right and take the old fire road northwest back to the junction with the Acadia Mountain Trail at 2.6 miles.

To return to the Island Explorer stop or the parking lot, continue straight on the Man o'War Brook Trail until it ends at the bus stop on ME 102 in another 0.1 mile. Turn left (south) onto the new spur trail to return to the parking lot in another 0.1 mile.

Miles and Directions

0.0 From the trailhead across from the parking lot, turn immediately left onto a new spur trail paralleling ME 102 that takes you to the Island Explorer bus stop.

0.1 From the bus stop head east into the woods on the gravel Man o' War Brook Trail, an old fire road.

0.2 Pick up the Acadia Mountain Trail on the left (north) side of the gravel Man o' War Brook Trail, across from the junction with the St. Sauveur Trail.

0.8 Reach the Acadia Mountain summit.

1.1 Reach a secondary summit.

1.7 At the junction with the spur to Man o' War Brook Trail and the spur to Man o' War Brook, turn left (east) to the brook.

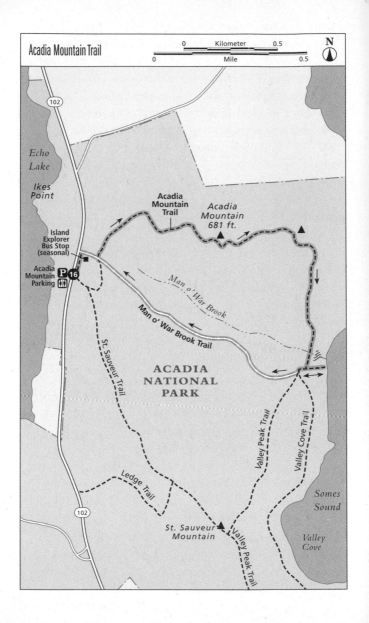

Acadia Mountain Trail

0   Kilometer   0.5

0   Mile   0.5

N

Echo Lake

Ikes Point

Island Explorer Bus Stop (seasonal)

Acadia Mountain Parking

P 16

Acadia Mountain Trail

Acadia Mountain 681 ft.

Man o' War Brook

Man o' War Brook Trail

ACADIA NATIONAL PARK

St. Sauveur Trail

Ledge Trail

St. Sauveur Mountain

Valley Peak Trail

Valley Peak Trail

Valley Cove Trail

Somes Sound

Valley Cove

102

102

1.8 Reach Man o' War Brook.

1.9 Return to the junction with the spur trail to Man o' War Brook Trail and head straight (west) to another major trail junction, where you bear right (northwest) to follow the old fire road.

2.6 Reach the junction with the Acadia Mountain Trail. Stay straight on the old fire road.

2.7 Reach the Island Explorer bus stop on ME 102. Turn left (south) onto the spur trail paralleling ME 102.

2.8 Arrive back at the parking lot.

17 Flying Mountain Trail

This hike takes you up the lowest of twenty-six peaks in Acadia, yet it features one of the best panoramas, overlooking Somes Sound, Fernald Cove, and the Cranberry Isles. There are views of Acadia and Norumbega Mountains, as well as excellent access to a large beach under the cliffs at Valley Cove, where you might even see peregrine falcons in flight.

Distance: 1.4-mile loop
Approximate hiking time: 1 hour
Difficulty: Moderate
Trail surface: Forest floor, rock ledges, gravel road
Best season: Spring through fall, particularly early morning and late afternoon in the summer to avoid the crowds
Other trail users: Boaters and kayakers coming ashore in Valley Cove for day hikes, birders

Canine compatibility: Leashed dogs permitted but not recommended because of some steep sections
Nat Geo Trails Illustrated Topographic Map: Acadia National Park
Special considerations: No facilities

Finding the trailhead: From Somesville head south on ME 102 for about 4.5 miles, past the St. Sauveur Mountain parking lot. Turn left (east) onto Fernald Point Road and travel about 1 mile to the small parking area at the foot of the gravel Valley Cove Trail, an old fire road. The trailhead is on the right (east) side of the parking area. The Island Explorer bus does not stop here. **GPS:** N44 17.57' / W68 18.55'

The Hike

It's easy to see how Flying Mountain got its name, from the way the trail ascends swiftly to a bird's-eye view. In just 0.3 mile from the parking area, you reach the 284-foot summit and its dramatic vistas.

The trail, first described in the late 1800s, climbs through deep woods and then up rocky ledges. While in the shade of the woods, hikers should be pleased that the Park Service several years ago improved this old and well-trodden trail by adding log cribbing, or interlocked logs, to support the steep climb. We counted ninety-three newer log steps right at the start of the ascent. The work helps prevent erosion and makes it an easier climb for children and others. Soon granite ledges serve as stone steps, sometimes interspersed with cribbing.

Once above tree line and at the top of the rock face, you get views to the southeast of Greening Island and the Cranberry Isles. To the northwest are the rocky cliffs of Valley Peak. Dominating the view from the summit is the grassy peninsula known as Fernald Point. Across the Narrows at the mouth of Somes Sound is the town of Northeast Harbor. From here you can look down on kayakers rounding Fernald Point or boaters entering and leaving Somes Sound. You may even hear a ferry blow its whistle in Northeast Harbor, as we did on one of our climbs here.

Some hikers turn around here, content with the views on Flying Mountain. But those who go on are rewarded with scenes of Somes Sound; Valley Cove; and Norumbega, Acadia, Penobscot, and Sargent Mountains. Some may even be fortunate enough to see or hear peregrine falcons, which have returned to nesting in the cliffs above Valley Cove, one of Acadia's top conservation accomplishments.

"It's a feel-good story," said Bruce Connery, recently retired wildlife biologist at Acadia. "It is positive, positive, positive."

Peregrine falcons nearly became extinct in the 1960s, but Rachel Carson's book *Silent Spring* alarmed the public and helped push the federal government to ban the pesticide DDT, which can dangerously thin eggshells, and pass the Endangered Species Act in 1972.

The park reintroduced peregrine falcons, and the first successful nest in thirty-five years occurred in 1991. Since then, more than 140 peregrine falcon chicks have fledged in the park, mainly at Valley Cove, Jordan Cliffs, and the precipice on the east face of Champlain Mountain. Acadia still runs an active banding program for the chicks.

The Flying Mountain Trail is noted for bird watching, including for falcons, osprey, and songbirds. On a recent hike, we took photos of a black-throated green warbler in the woods just off the peak and spotted a falcon soaring high above.

Just beyond the summit of Flying Mountain, at 0.4 mile, you get the first glimpse of the northern reaches of Somes Sound, as well as of Acadia Mountain to the north and Norumbega Mountain on the other side of the sound to the northeast. The ridge of Sargent and Penobscot Mountains is just beyond that of Norumbega. There's a spur to an overlook to the right (east) before the trail begins its steep descent toward Valley Cove.

When the trail reaches the shore of the cove, go left (west). A new wooden bridge with a railing crosses a stream and separate hard-surface steps on each end converge at a short, wide stairway that provides excellent access down to the rocky cove and pebble beach. There's lots of room,

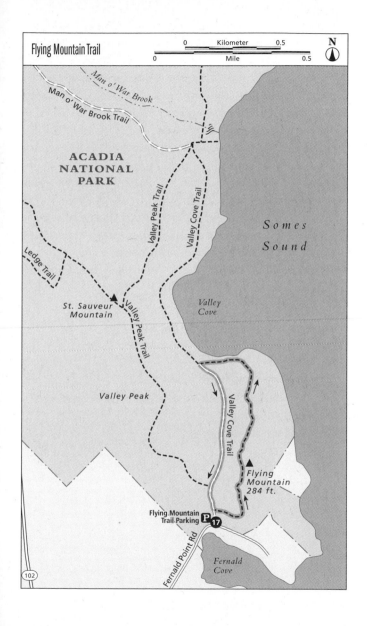

Flying Mountain Trail

ACADIA NATIONAL PARK

Man o' War Brook

Man o' War Brook Trail

Valley Peak Trail

Valley Cove Trail

Ledge Trail

Somes Sound

St. Sauveur Mountain

Valley Cove

Valley Peak Trail

Valley Peak

Valley Cove Trail

Flying Mountain 284 ft.

Flying Mountain Trail Parking

P 17

Fernald Point Rd

Fernald Cove

102

Kilometer

Mile

especially at low tide, and great views of steep, dark cliffs rising above the sound, and of herring gulls soaring nearby.

The beach access was part of a rehabilitation in 2016 after the trail was damaged during the winter. In addition to two new wooden bridges, the work included more than 425 feet of new tread surface on the Flying Mountain Trail and new stone and log retaining walls.

At about 0.9 mile you reach the junction with the gravel Valley Cove Trail, an old fire road. Turn left (south) onto the old fire road and loop back to the parking area at 1.4 miles. Hardy hikers can stay straight along the rocky shores of Valley Cove and add on a more challenging 1-mile section of the Valley Cove Trail that heads north, if it's not closed for peregrine falcon nesting season. A major upgrade of the Valley Cove Trail began in 2018 and should be finished by 2019.

Miles and Directions

0.0 Start at the Flying Mountain trailhead, on the east side of the parking area at the foot of the gravel Valley Cove Trail (an old fire road).

0.3 Reach the summit of Flying Mountain.

0.9 Turn left at the junction with Valley Cove Trail to loop back to the parking area.

1.4 Arrive back at the trailhead.

18 Beech Cliff Loop Trail

Enjoy cliff-top views of Echo Lake and beyond from this easy trail featuring a loop and out–and–back section. You can see the fire tower on nearby Beech Mountain from a rocky knob. From spring to midsummer peregrine falcons may be nesting in the cliffs below the trail.

Distance: 0.6-mile lollipop
Approximate hiking time: 30 minutes to 1 hour
Difficulty: Easy
Trail surface: Forest floor, graded gravel path, rock ledges
Best season: Spring through fall, particularly early morning or late afternoon in the summer to avoid the crowds

Other trail users: Hikers going to the Canada Cliff Trail or coming up a difficult ladder climb from Echo Lake
Canine compatibility: Leashed dogs permitted
Nat Geo Trails Illustrated Topographic Map: Acadia National Park
Special considerations: Portable toilets at parking lot

Finding the trailhead: Head south from Somesville on ME 102 and turn right (west) at the flashing yellow light toward Pretty Marsh. Take the second left onto Beech Hill Road, at a sign pointing to Beech Mountain and Beech Cliff. Follow Beech Hill Road south for 3.2 miles to the parking lot at its end. The trailhead is across the parking lot, on the left (east) side of the road. The Island Explorer bus does not stop here, although the Southwest Harbor line lets off at Echo Lake, which is a difficult ladder climb away that is not recommended for the out of shape or faint of heart, and is not allowed for dogs. **GPS:** N44 18.55' / W68 20.36'

The Hike

This is the easier of two ways to access Beech Cliff and its views, because the trailhead is basically at the same elevation as the cliff. (The other way is a difficult ladder climb up Beech Cliff from Echo Lake.)

From the parking lot the trail rises gradually through the woods to a junction with the Canada Cliff Trail at 0.1 mile. Bear left (northeast) to the Beech Cliff Loop, where you have a choice of taking the inland or the cliff side of the loop. Either way is relatively flat, with some granite steps to make the footing easier, but we prefer getting the views first: Bear right for the cliff side of the loop, reaching Beech Cliff at 0.2 mile.

From Beech Cliff you can look down on Echo Lake Beach and the Appalachian Mountain Club (AMC) camp—but do not get too close to the edge. Acadia and St. Sauveur Mountains are farther east. To the south are Somes Sound, the Gulf of Maine, and the Cranberry Isles. And to the southwest is Beech Mountain, with its fire tower. You may also hear the traffic on ME 102, across the lake.

The trail continues along the cliff, then circles inland, closing the loop at 0.5 mile. Bear right (southwest) to return to the parking lot at 0.6 mile.

Miles and Directions

0.0   Start at the Beech Cliff Loop trailhead, across the road (east) from the parking lot.

0.1   At the junction with Canada Cliff Trail, bear left (northeast) to the Beech Cliff Loop Trail, where you can take the cliff side of the loop first (right) or the inland side (left).

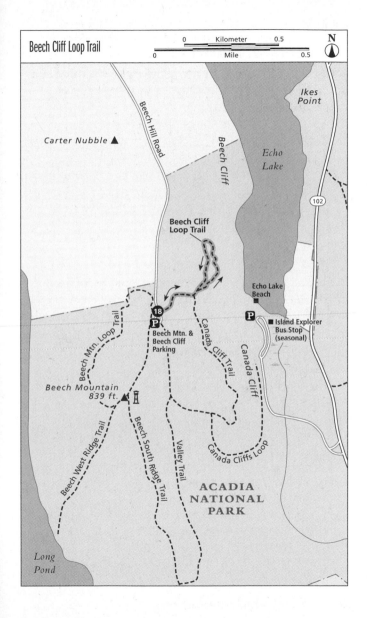

0.2 Reach Beech Cliff, if you take the cliff side of the loop first. If you take the inland side of the loop first, it'll be slightly longer before you reach the cliff's edge.

0.5 Circle back to close the loop at the junction with Canada Cliff Trail, and bear right (southwest) back to the parking lot.

0.6 Arrive back at the trailhead.

19 Beech Mountain Loop Trail

This hike offers great views of Long Pond and Somes Sound, along with a chance to climb to either the lower or top platform of the park's only fire tower, a steel structure, still in good condition, atop 839-foot Beech Mountain. The trail is also a good place for bird watching, including the migration of hawks; we saw four kestrels dive and soar above us during a hike one fall.

Distance: 1.1-mile loop
Approximate hiking time: 1 hour
Difficulty: Moderate
Trail surface: Forest floor, graded gravel path, rock ledges
Best season: Spring through fall
Other trail users: Hikers coming from the Beech South Ridge or Beech West Ridge Trails, birders

Canine compatibility: Leashed dogs permitted
Nat Geo Trails Illustrated Topographic Map: Acadia National Park
Special considerations: Portable toilets at parking lot

Finding the trailhead: Head south from Somesville on ME 102 and turn right (west) at the flashing yellow light toward Pretty Marsh. Take the second left onto Beech Hill Road, at a sign pointing to Beech Mountain and Beech Cliff. Follow Beech Hill Road south for 3.2 miles to the parking lot at its end. The trailhead is at the northwest end of the parking lot. The Island Explorer bus does not stop here, although the Southwest Harbor line lets people off at Echo Lake, a very steep climb away up a ladder trail. **GPS:** N44 18.54' / W68 20.37'

The Hike

A must-hike in Acadia, Beech Mountain rises from a thin peninsula-like ridge of land sandwiched between Long Pond and Echo Lake, providing views all around. And if you happen to hike Beech Mountain late one afternoon, you may be treated to a sunset that rivals the one you can get from Cadillac.

The trail begins off the parking lot and quickly leads to a loop at 0.1 mile.

The western half of this loop was carved in the 1960s as part of "Mission 66," an overhaul effort by the Park Service to celebrate its fiftieth anniversary in 1966. The trail's eastern section is much older, appearing on a 1906 map, according to *Pathmakers*, a report by the Park Service's Olmsted Center for Landscape Preservation.

Bear right (northwest) at the fork to head along the easier Mission 66 way (counterclockwise) around the loop up to the summit. You soon get spectacular views of Long Pond to the right (west) of the wide-open trail. At 0.6 mile you reach the junction with the Beech West Ridge Trail. Bear left (east). A series of log stairs leads to the summit.

At 0.7 mile you reach the steel fire tower atop Beech Mountain and the junction with the Beech South Ridge Trail. From the fire tower's first platform, which is always open, you can enjoy nearly 360-degree views of the ocean and surrounding mountains. Echo Lake, Acadia Mountain, and St. Sauveur Mountain are to the east, while Southwest Harbor, Northeast Harbor, and the Cranberry Isles are to the southeast and Long Pond is to the west.

Several years ago, the park launched a new program that involves opening the top platform of the fire tower for

2-hour periods at certain times and days during the summer and fall. The "fire tower open houses" are staffed by a ranger, and the schedule is available on the park's online calendar of upcoming events or by calling the park at (207) 288-3338.

Gary Stellpflug, trails foreman at Acadia National Park, said he is pleased to see the opening of the top catwalk, which provides even more sweeping views of the region. Stellpflug said the Beech Mountain fire tower is among a declining number of such towers that people can safely go up and down.

"It's a wonderful place," he said. "Everyone wants to go up there. It's cool."

The fire tower's cabin, however, remains closed. The cabin has a wooden floor, unlike the steel grating on the platforms, and may not be safe.

According to the Park Service, the fire tower was originally wooden, built around 1937 to 1941 by the Civilian Conservation Corps. It was replaced around 1960 to 1962 with a prefabricated steel tower flown in by helicopter and assembled on-site as part of the Mission 66 move to improve the parks. The Park Service last staffed the tower, which is on the National Historic Lookout Register, in 1976.

From the summit bear left (north) at the junction with the Beech South Ridge Trail and loop back down quickly along the rough mountain face. Descend along switchbacks, open cliff face, and through boulder fields. Go down a series of stone steps and then log steps. Bear right (southeast) at a fork at 1.0 mile and return to the parking area at 1.1 miles.

Miles and Directions

0.0   Start at the Beech Mountain Loop trailhead, at the northwest corner of the parking lot.

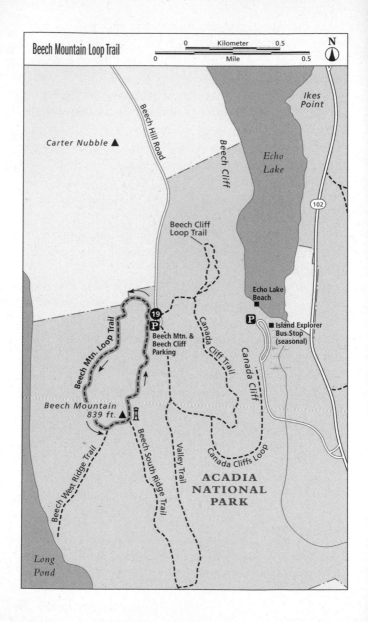

Beech Mountain Loop Trail

0 Kilometer 0.5
0 Mile 0.5

N

Carter Nubble ▲

Beech Hill Road

Beech Cliff

Ikes Point

Echo Lake

102

Beech Cliff Loop Trail

Echo Lake Beach

P

19
P
Beech Mtn. & Beech Cliff Parking

Island Explorer Bus Stop (seasonal)

Beech Mtn. Loop Trail

Canada Cliff Trail

Canada Cliff

Beech Mountain 839 ft. ▲

Beech West Ridge Trail

Beech South Ridge Trail

Valley Trail

Canada Cliffs Loop

ACADIA NATIONAL PARK

Long Pond

0.1 Bear right (northwest) at the fork, going around the loop counterclockwise.

0.6 At the junction with the Beech West Ridge Trail, bear left (east) to circle up Beech Mountain.

0.7 Reach the Beech Mountain summit. Bear left (north) at the junction with the Beech South Ridge Trail to circle back down the mountain.

1.0 Bear right (southeast) at the fork.

1.1 Arrive back at the trailhead.

20 Wonderland

This very easy trail along an old road brings you to pink-granite outcrops along the shore and tide pools at low tide. You will see skunk cabbage, pitch pine, and wild sarsaparilla along the way, and ponder why broken-up mussel shells are found inland along the trail rather than on the coastline.

Distance: 1.4 miles out and back

Approximate hiking time: 1 hour

Difficulty: Easy

Trail surface: Graded gravel road

Best season: Spring through fall, particularly early morning or late afternoon in the summer to avoid the crowds; low tide for tidal pool exploration

Other trail users: Birders

Canine compatibility: Leashed dogs permitted

Nat Geo Trails Illustrated Topographic Map: Acadia National Park

Special considerations: Wheelchair accessible with assistance; closest facilities at Seawall picnic area or Ship Harbor Trail

Finding the trailhead: From Southwest Harbor head south about 1 mile on ME 102. Bear left (southeast) on ME 102A, passing the town of Manset in about 1 mile and Seawall Campground and picnic area in about 3 miles and reaching the Wonderland trailhead in about 4 miles. Parking is on the left (southeast) side of the road. The trail heads southeast along an abandoned gravel road toward the shore. The Island Explorer's Southwest Harbor line stops at Seawall Campground, a mile away, and passes by Wonderland on the way to Bass Harbor Campground. You may want to ask if the bus driver will let you off at the Wonderland parking area. **GPS:** N44 14.01' / W68 19.12'

The Hike

Walk through the diverse forest, see the smooth pink granite along the shore and the birds, smell the salty sea, and explore the tide pools, and you will know why they call this Wonderland.

The easy trail along an old gravel road starts by winding through dark woods, including tall and feathery tamarack, a deciduous conifer that loses its needles in the fall; and then by wild sarsaparilla, which is thick in the ground cover, and cinnamon fern.

At about 0.1 mile go up a slight hill and make your way carefully among some roots and rocks. This is the toughest part of an otherwise gentle, well-graded trail.

During a "Birds and Botany of Wonderland" tour, Susan Hayward, a founder of the Maine Master Naturalist Program, pointed out flowers such as beach pea and black chokeberry, and woody plants like alder, shadbush, and a large mat of broom crowberry. She stopped next to some tall pitch pine, which is uncommon farther north of Acadia and has more needles per cluster and larger cones than jack pine, fairly common north and west of Acadia.

"Pitch pine is rare in this part of the woods," Hayward said. "It has a bundle of three needles per cluster," while jack pine has two.

Through the trees you begin to see the ocean on the right (southeast). At 0.7 mile the trail brings you to the shore, where the pink granite dramatically meets the sea. You can spend hours exploring here, especially when low tide exposes a bar to Long Ledge and tide pools with their diverse marine life, from rockweed to barnacles to green crabs. Be careful of wet rocks, slick seaweed, and sudden waves.

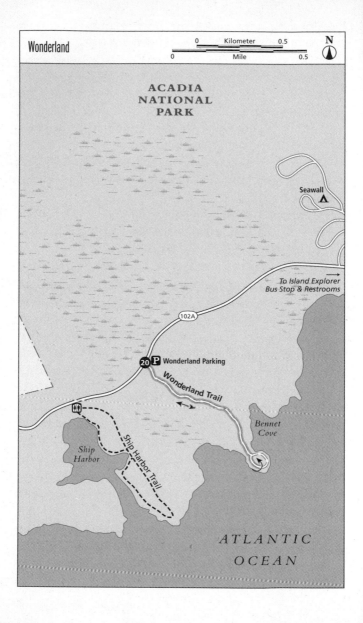

Attending the annual Acadia Birding Festival, we were amazed to look through a scope and watch a flock of about three dozen black scoters diving headfirst into the ocean for food and then fluttering their wings upon emerging.

We also spotted an adult bald eagle, with its trademark white head and tail; a red-breasted nuthatch hopping on limbs; and songbirds such as a black-throated green warbler and a yellow-rumped warbler.

You can also take forever and a day to explore inland along the trail, as our nieces Sharon and Michelle did when we hiked this together, wondering about cracked-up seashells and seaweed found far from shore. We theorized that gulls must have dropped the mussel shells from midair to open them for food. That was proven later in the trip when we hiked the Bar Island Trail at low tide and witnessed that same gull-feeding activity. There are many things to wonder about along Wonderland.

Return the way you came.

Miles and Directions

0.0 Start at the Wonderland trailhead, on the southeast side of ME 102A, at the edge of the parking area.

0.1 The trail heads slightly uphill.

0.7 Reach the shoreline, where you can add on a loop to explore the rocky outcroppings.

1.4 Arrive back at the trailhead.

21 Ship Harbor Trail

With a maritime mystery in its past, a huge undeveloped harbor, and sprawling pink granite, the Ship Harbor Trail epitomizes a lot about hiking the coast of Acadia National Park. President Barack Obama chose the trail as one of only a few he hiked with his wife and daughters during a visit in July 2010.

Distance: 1.3-mile figure-eight loop

Approximate hiking time: 1 hour

Difficulty: Easy

Trail surface: Graded gravel path, forest floor, rocky shore

Best season: Spring through fall, particularly early morning or late afternoon in the summer to avoid the crowds; low tide to explore tidal pools

Other trail users: Visitors with wheelchairs or baby strollers

Canine compatibility: Leashed dogs permitted

Nat Geo Trails Illustrated Topographic Map: Acadia National Park

Special considerations: The first 0.25 mile of the trail is on a hard-packed surface, making it accessible to visitors with wheelchairs or baby strollers. There is a chemical toilet at the trailhead.

Finding the trailhead: From Southwest Harbor head south about 1 mile on ME 102. Bear left (southeast) on ME 102A, passing the town of Manset in about 1 mile, Seawall Campground and picnic area in about 3 miles, and the Wonderland Trail parking area in about 4 miles. The Ship Harbor trailhead is about 0.2 mile beyond Wonderland. The trailhead parking lot is on the left (south) side of ME 102A. The Island Explorer's Southwest Harbor line stops at Seawall Campground more than a mile away and passes by Ship Harbor Trail on the way to Bass Harbor Campground. You may want to ask if the bus driver will let you off at the Ship Harbor Trail parking area. **GPS:** N44 13.54' / W68 19.31'

The Hike

The trail is one of the easiest and most popular in Acadia, maybe because it offers so much: a thick spruce forest, wild-flowers and lowbush blueberries in season, expanses of flat granite for relaxing next to the surf, intimate views of the islands, and the drama of the sea crashing against immense cliffs.

Located on the southern shore of the west side of Mount Desert Island, the hike is comprised of two loops, or a figure eight, totaling 1.3 miles with colorful, new wayside exhibits that explain sea life in the flats and tide pools.

The history of Ship Harbor and the trail is also fascinating.

The name of the harbor may stretch back to the fall of 1739, when some believe it was the site of the wreck of the *Grand Design*, an English vessel carrying Irish immigrants to Pennsylvania. A park-wide archaeological study in 2004 found evidence that suggests the name of the harbor may stem from that disaster, though there is no definitive proof.

The trail itself took decades to reach fruition.

Park pioneers George B. Dorr and John D. Rockefeller Jr. worked to provide roadside access to Ship Harbor as early as the 1930s, and it was queued up to be completed by the Civilian Conservation Corps, but the work was left undone when the Corps disbanded in the park at the onset of World War II. It was finally completed in 1957 as part of a national program to improve the National Park System in time for its fiftieth anniversary in 1966.

Important new work was finished in 2015, when the entire first, or inner, 0.6-mile loop was improved and regraded to comply with access standards for physically disabled people, according to Gary Stellpflug, Acadia trails foreman.

During the hike, when you reach the first fork, at 0.1 mile at the base of the figure-eight loop, bear right (south), following the hard-packed surface to the edge of the Ship Harbor channel and the mudflats, which can be viewed at low tide. The trail now begins to get rocky and uneven as it approaches an intersection at 0.3 mile, in the middle of the figure-eight loop. Bear right along the graded surface to the edge of the Ship Harbor channel.

At low tide, the mudflats on the channel are ideal for exploring, as we did on a hike with our nieces Sharon and Michelle.

Common eiders are often seen floating at the mouth of Ship Harbor, and it's possible to catch glimpses along the trail of a bald eagle or osprey, or even of such uncommon birds as a palm warbler or an olive-sided flycatcher. At 0.7 mile, near the mouth of Ship Harbor, you reach the rocky shore along the Atlantic. Here you can admire the dramatic pink cliffs or explore tidal pools at low tide, when barnacles, rockweed, snails, and other sea life are exposed by the receding waters. Granite cliffs stretch to the edge of the ocean shore at the tip of this loop.

Turn left to circle back along the remaining section of the figure-eight loop. When you reach an intersection at 1.0 mile, back at the center of the figure-eight loop, bear right (northwest) to continue along the hilly inland section of the loop, which is now well-graded and accessible. Or, if you are tempted to return along the Ship Harbor channel, you can bear left at this intersection instead, to retrace your steps along the channel northwest back to the trailhead.

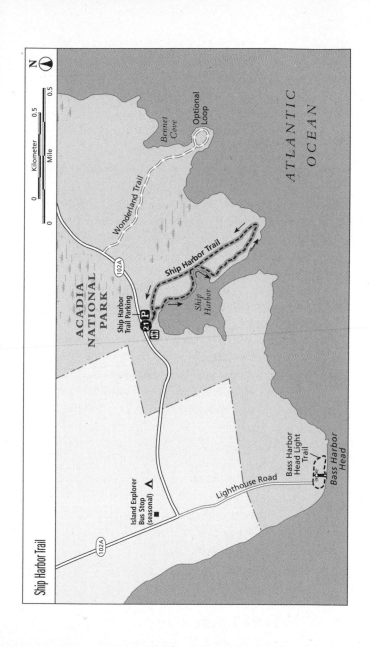

At a fork at the base of the figure-eight loop, bear north-west for 0.1 mile to return to the parking lot. You will walk over almost 300 feet of bogwalk, constructed with three planks instead of the usual two, to help protect the fragile area from heavy use.

Miles and Directions

0.0 Start at the Ship Harbor trailhead, on the left (south) side of ME 102A.

0.1 Bear right (south) at the fork, at the base of the figure-eight loop, and head along the edge of the Ship Harbor channel.

0.3 At the intersection in the middle of the figure-eight loop, bear right again to continue along the edge of the Ship Harbor channel.

0.7 Reach the rocky shoreline along the Atlantic and turn left (northwest) to circle back along the hilly inland section of the figure-eight loop.

1.0 At the intersection in the middle of the figure-eight loop, bear right (northwest) to continue along the hilly inland section.

1.2 Reach the fork at the base of the figure-eight loop and bear right (northwest) to head back to the parking lot.

1.3 Arrive back at the trailhead.

22 Bass Harbor Head Light Trail

Get a close-up view of the only lighthouse on Mount Desert Island, which uses a 1,000-watt red beacon to guide lobster boats and other mariners safely over the shoals to Bass Harbor. On one side of the parking lot, stairs bring you down the steep bluff to an overlook that provides views not only of Bass Harbor Head Light but also of Blue Hill Bay and Swans Island. On the other side, follow a paved path to stand under the lighthouse and read displays about its history.

Distance: 0.4 mile out and back
Approximate hiking time: 30 minutes
Difficulty: Moderate
Trail surface: Wooden deck and stairs, graded gravel path, rock ledges and steps, paved walkway
Best season: Spring through fall, particularly early morning or late afternoon in the summer to avoid the crowds
Other trail users: None
Canine compatibility: Leashed dogs permitted

Nat Geo Trails Illustrated Topographic Map: Acadia National Park
Special considerations: There is a chemical toilet at the edge of the parking lot near the trailhead. The automated lighthouse is not open to the public, and neither is the former lighthouse keeper's house. Hike the trail only in safe conditions; that is, not when it's stormy or when surf is crashing against the cliffs.

Finding the trailhead: From Bass Harbor head south about 0.6 mile on ME 102A until you reach a sharp curve in the road, where ME 102A heads left (east). Go straight ahead (south) on the 0.5-mile dead-end Lighthouse Road that takes you to the Bass Harbor Head Light parking lot. The trail begins on the left (southeastern) edge of the parking lot, across from the toilets. The Island Explorer bus does not stop here, although the Southwest Harbor line has a Bass Harbor Campground stop near the beginning of the dead-end road to the lighthouse. **GPS:** N44 13.21' / W68 20.13'

The Hike

Maine is synonymous with not only lobster but also lighthouses.

More than sixty towering beacons still stand guard along the state's 3,500 miles of rocky coastline, with perhaps one of the most photogenic being Bass Harbor Head Light in Acadia National Park. Certainly the contrast of Acadia's distinctive pink granite against the lighthouse's white tower makes for a picture-postcard view, and many visitors come to create a picture of their own.

Built in 1858, the lighthouse, originally lit with a brass lamp fired by whale oil, even today directs boaters safely in and out of Bass Harbor and Blue Hill Bay with its red beacon that was automated in 1974.

The National Park Service, which owns lighthouses on Bear Island and Baker Island in the park, also agreed in 2017 to take ownership of Bass Harbor Head Light from the US Coast Guard and was considering possible uses in 2018.

The trail is split into two 0.2-mile sections on either side of the light station, and each offers revealing views and different experiences.

On the southeastern edge of the parking lot across from the toilets, head southeast along the trail through the woods to a wooden staircase. Go down the steep stairs, and loop back along the rocks toward the lighthouse to an overlook. The length of this section of trail, only 0.1 mile one-way to the overlook, makes it seem easy, but its steepness, even if on wooden stairs, makes it moderately difficult Take your time. Let the stunning views take your breath away, and not overexertion.

From the overlook the view includes Bass Harbor Head Light, the ocean, and outlying islands, including Swans Island, which has a year-round population serviced by a vehicle ferry from Bass Harbor.

If you clamber along the rocks to get different perspectives, as our nieces did on a trip here, be careful. The rocks can be slippery, especially when wet.

Return the way you came, then cross the parking lot to pick up the trail on the other side of the lighthouse.

The trail on the southwestern edge of the lot allows visitors to stand under the 32-foot-high lighthouse, touch its white-brick exterior, and view two shipshape bells while enjoying scenic views of the ocean and the craggy cliffs below.

Along the 0.1-mile paved path are some enlightening educational exhibits. Stop and read displays about key dates in the history of the light station, details of its ten-sided lantern, and the proper care of a fog bell and other recurring and demanding duties of a lighthouse keeper.

Bass Harbor Head Light can be jam-packed, especially on a nice summer weekend close to sunset. But former President Barack Obama toured it during his vacation at the park in July 2010, and maybe you should too.

Return the way you came.

Miles and Directions

0.0 Start at the Bass Harbor Head Light trailhead, on the left (southeastern) edge of the parking lot.

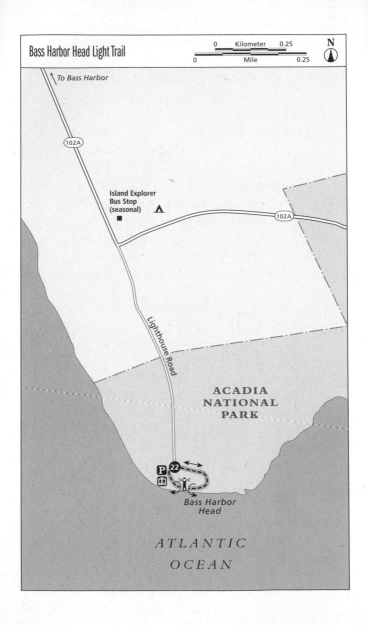

Bass Harbor Head Light Trail

0   Kilometer   0.25

0   Mile   0.25

N

To Bass Harbor

102A

Island Explorer
Bus Stop
(seasonal)

102A

Lighthouse Road

ACADIA
NATIONAL
PARK

P

22

Bass Harbor
Head

ATLANTIC
OCEAN

0.1 Reach the overlook at the end of the wooden stairs and rock path, with views of Bass Harbor Head Light, Blue Hill Bay, and outlying islands.

0.2 Arrive back at the parking lot and cross to pick up a paved path on the northwestern edge of the lot.

0.3 Reach the western side of the lighthouse.

0.4 Arrive back at the trailhead.

Hike Index

About the Authors

Dolores Kong and Dan Ring have backpacked all of the more than 270 miles of the Appalachian Trail in Maine and have climbed virtually all the peaks that are 4,000 feet and higher in the Northeast. They are members of the White Mountains Four Thousand Footer, the New England Four Thousand Footer, the Adirondack 46Rs, the Northeast 111ers, and the New England Hundred Highest Clubs.

Dolores is a Certified Financial Planner™ professional and senior vice president with Winslow, Evans & Crocker, Inc. (member of FINRA/SIPC), in Boston. A Barnard College graduate, she is also a Pulitzer Prize finalist in public service from her previous career as a staff writer at the *Boston Globe*.

Dan is an operations professional with Winslow, Evans & Crocker, Inc. (member of FINRA/SIPC), in Boston, and a writer who has been a statehouse bureau chief in Boston for a variety of newspapers. He graduated from Boston College with a bachelor's degree in English. Dan and Dolores are married and live outside Boston. They write a blog, acadiaonmymind.com.